EAT AT HOME
TONIGHT

101 *Simple* Busy-Family Recipes for Your Slow Cooker, Sheet Pan, Instant Pot®, and More

TIFFANY KING

WATERBROOK

*For Mom, thank you for cooking more family dinners
than can be counted. And for Dad, your presence at
the end of the table and prayers at the beginning of the
meal have shaped our family for the better.*

EAT AT HOME TONIGHT
Hardcover ISBN 978-0-7352-9123-2
eBook ISBN 978-0-7352-9124-9

Published in the United States by
WaterBrook, an imprint of the Crown
Publishing Group, a division of Penguin
Random House LLC, New York.

WATERBROOK® and its deer colophon are
registered trademarks of Penguin Random
House LLC.

Library of Congress Cataloging-in-
Publication Data

Names: King, Tiffany, 1967– author.
Title: Eat at home tonight: 101 simple busy-
family recipes for your slow cooker, sheet pan,
Instant Pot, and more/Tiffany King.
Description: First edition. | New York:
WaterBrook, an imprint of the Crown
Publishing Group, a division of Penguin, 2018.
Identifiers: LCCN 2017048917| ISBN
9780735291232 (hardcover) | ISBN
9780735291249 (ebook)
Subjects: LCSH: Cooking, American. | Quick
and easy cooking. | Dinners and dining. |
LCGFT: Cookbooks.
Classification: LCC TX737 .K564 2018 | DDC
641.5/12—dc23
LC record available at
https://lccn.loc.gov/2017048917.

Printed in China

2018—First Edition

10 9 8 7 6 5 4 3 2 1

SPECIAL SALES

Most WaterBrook books are available at
special quantity discounts when purchased
in bulk by corporations, organizations, and
special-interest groups. Custom imprinting
or excerpting can also be done to fit special
needs. For information, please e-mail
specialmarketscms@penguinrandomhouse.com
or call 1-800-603-7051.

CONTENTS

INTRODUCTION

—

I love dinnertime, but it's not always easy to pull off. Dinner comes with many challenges. From trying to cook while holding a cranky baby to figuring out how to prep a meal while simultaneously driving a preteen across town to soccer practice, this part of parenting stretches us and tempts us to throw in the towel on a homemade meal.

I've been gathering my family around the table since before our kids were born. When Jim and I married thirty years ago, we had dinner together each night. Meals were humble because we had no money and didn't really know how to cook. But those dinners laid the foundation of our marriage and family.

In the years since, I've cooked with babies on my hip, toddlers underfoot, and preschoolers who wanted to help. I've cooked for picky kids, juggled conflicting schedules, struggled in years when we lacked money, and learned to cook quickly in the years when I lacked time.

Most of those family dinners run together in my memory. There are very few that I have specific memories of, but they all worked together to build strong bonds among the six of us. Now that my kids are all grown or nearly grown, we continue to see the benefits of all those dinners. We still start meals by holding hands and praying together. We still gather around the table. Sometimes there are only three of us there, but about once a week we're able to get all eight of us together—including the spouses of our two oldest kids. The young married couples have continued the dinner tradition in their homes, too, building that habit with each other.

Despite the challenges, dinner offers benefits that no other hour can provide. In his bestselling book *The Five Love Languages*, Gary Chapman asserts that all of us have a primary love language, meaning we feel love best when it's expressed in one of five ways: quality time, physical touch, words of affirmation, acts of service, or gift giving. I think dinner is the only time during the day that we can hit all five love languages for our family members. Taking time together to sit and share with each other meets the love language of quality time. Holding hands around the table while we pray provides physical touch. Conversation during the meal about how our days have gone is a foundation for us to give words of affirmation to each other. Cooking the meal, clearing the table after dinner, or offering to clean up are all acts of service. While gift giving might be a stretch during a regular dinner, making a favorite meal for a family member is a gift to that person.

Dinner together makes all of us feel love in the way we feel it best. And isn't showing love for each other one of the best ways to grow a strong family? There's something special about knowing we each have a place at the table. Seeing family members gathered at dinner provides a visual security of who each person is in the family and how they fit, both in the family and around the table.

Dinner also gives us a built-in opportunity to pray together as a family. There's something sacred about holding hands around the table and bowing our heads together. Even though on some nights, this is done quickly and maybe with little thought, it's such a special time together. Those few moments are a chance to practice gratefulness together as well as an opportunity to pray about things that weigh on our hearts.

My hope for you is that you will build the dinner habit into your family life so your connections with each other grow stronger. I can almost hear you saying, "But there are so many challenges that come with this! Sometimes it seems our schedules and outside demands conspire against us." That's where this book comes in. Each chapter is designed to solve a different challenge you might face on any given night. From needing a one-pot meal because you lack time to do the dishes to being out of the house all day without time for cooking to only having fifteen minutes to pull dinner together, you'll find recipes that will fit your busy days.

Make this book your own by writing notes in it as you try the recipes. Jot down how your family liked each meal and any substitutions or changes you made or would like to make the next time you cook the recipe. Make notes on which meals worked well for after church on Sunday, or those for which you want to keep the ingredients on hand for quick meals when plan A falls through. If you live in a high-altitude area, you may need to make adjustments to baking and pressure-cooking times, so be sure to make note of those, too.

Dinner together can be hard. It involves teaching toddlers to sit at the table, convincing kids to try new foods, and much juggling of schedules to carve out time for a meal together. But when we build the habit of gathering around the table night after night, strong family bonds are forged. And the benefits of those bonds carry on to future generations in ways we may never know.

I ONLY HAVE 15 MINUTES TONIGHT

I started creating recipes that could be finished in fifteen minutes when my oldest kids were teens. Life had suddenly gotten very busy, and I more often found myself in the car taxiing kids to practice than in the kitchen making dinner. All those hours of shuttling to and fro don't leave much time for dinner-making, or anything else.

I found we were often ravenous when we finally got home, and if I hadn't filled the slow cooker earlier in the day, it meant dinner would be a scramble. It didn't take me long to put creative juices to work figuring out shortcuts to quick meals.

A quarter of an hour isn't much time, but I promise you that with a little strategy and some quick work, you can get dinner on the table for your family faster than the time it would take to run through a drive-through. It will be a lot less expensive, too!

Don't miss the section on cooking chicken for the freezer on page 133. Having meat already cooked and in the freezer is key for fifteen-minute meals. I have included some recipes for meals that don't require cooked chicken, but your options increase if you've got some stashed and waiting for you.

I also recommend a sharp knife. This is essential for any kitchen, but it becomes really important when you're working in a time crunch. You need a tool that will work well for you, not one that will fight you with every cut.

The next time you find yourself rushing into the house with no time for dinner-making, try one of these recipes. They'll keep you and your family happy and keep you out of the fast-food places, too.

TIME SAVING TIP My favorite way to speed up meal prep is to keep frozen cooked chicken handy. See page 133 for tips on how to cook chicken for the freezer.

Creamy Chicken Florentine Quesadillas

Serves 6 to 8

Quesadillas are a quintessential back-pocket recipe you can pull out when a dinner emergency strikes. But as much as we all love Tex-Mex, it's nice to have a change of pace sometimes. One run-of-the-mill day, I came up with these Florentine-inspired quesadillas. They're stuffed with whatever chicken you have on hand (from the local rotisserie or from your freezer stash) and made healthier with plenty of spinach and artichoke hearts. Cream cheese and Parmesan create a melty inside to contrast with the crisped outside. You can tailor them to even the pickiest eaters (trust me, I have a few). If you have persnickety little ones, too, just pull out the artichoke hearts. And yes, you can keep those extra artichokes all to yourself!

1 (8-ounce) package cream cheese, at room temperature (see note below)

1 teaspoon garlic powder

6 to 8 (8-inch) flour tortillas

Olive oil

3 cups chopped cooked chicken

1 (15-ounce) jar artichoke hearts, quartered

1 cup cherry tomatoes, or 1 large tomato, sliced

1 cup spinach

¼ cup shredded Parmesan cheese

ALL-IS-NOT-LOST WORKAROUND
Forgot to let your cream cheese come to room temperature beforehand? No worries! Unwrap the block of cream cheese and place it on a microwave-safe plate. Microwave for 15 seconds. It should be soft enough that your finger leaves a slight print when you lightly press the top. Add 10 seconds, if needed.

In a small bowl, stir together the cream cheese and garlic powder. Spread the cream cheese mixture over the tortillas.

Heat a medium skillet over medium heat. Add enough oil to coat the bottom of the pan. Place a tortilla in the skillet and divide the chicken, artichoke hearts, tomatoes, spinach, and Parmesan among the tortillas, arranging the filling over one half of each tortilla. Fold the half without fillings over to make a half-moon shape. Cook until the tortilla is browned and crisp, then gently flip and cook until the second side is browned and crisp. Repeat with the remaining tortillas.

Enjoy them while they're hot!

White Garlic Chicken Flatbread

Serves 6

"White Garlic Chicken Flatbread" may not sound very exciting, but I promise this recipe will not leave you missing the tomato sauce, pepperoni, or sausage that typically come with pizzas and flatbreads. This recipe grabs your attention with garlic and pepper (don't worry—it's not *too* spicy!) and then mellows out the taste with creamy mozzarella cheese. And the best part? Only fifteen minutes, start to finish!

1 tablespoon olive oil

½ cup diced onion

2 garlic cloves, crushed

2 tablespoons distilled white or cider vinegar

2 tablespoons soy sauce

⅛ teaspoon cayenne pepper

¼ teaspoon black pepper

1 tablespoon cornstarch

2½ cups shredded cooked chicken

6 mini naan, or 4 pita breads

2 cups shredded mozzarella cheese

Preheat the oven to 450°F.

In a large skillet, heat the olive oil over medium heat. Add the onion and garlic and cook, stirring, until the onion is soft, about 5 minutes. Stir the vinegar, soy sauce, cayenne, black pepper, cornstarch, and 1 tablespoon water together in a small bowl. Turn the heat off under the skillet and pour the vinegar mixture in with the onion and garlic, stirring to combine. Add the chicken to the skillet, tossing to combine it with the sauce.

Arrange the naan in a single layer on a baking sheet. Divide the chicken among the naan and top each with the cheese, dividing it evenly. Bake for 7 to 8 minutes, until the cheese melts and begins to brown. Serve hot.

Chicken Enchilada Melt Subs

Serves 6

When I first got married, I didn't know how to cook at all. Jim and I would get together with another married couple on the weekends, and we'd cook together. My friend taught me how to make easy chicken enchiladas during one of those cooking sessions. It's a recipe I use to this day because it uses basic pantry ingredients, so I almost always have what I need on hand. That recipe is quick, but it requires time to bake the enchiladas. Enter this sandwich version, which has all the cheesy goodness of a chicken enchilada but fits in a fifteen-minute time crunch.

3 cups shredded cooked chicken

1 (4-ounce) can diced green chiles, drained

1 (8-ounce) can tomato sauce

½ teaspoon garlic powder

Salt and black pepper

2 cups shredded cheddar cheese

6 sub rolls

Preheat the broiler.

In a large microwave-safe bowl, stir together the chicken, chiles, tomato sauce, and garlic powder and season with salt and pepper. Microwave the mixture for 2 minutes. Add 1 cup of the cheese and stir to combine.

Split the sub rolls horizontally and set them cut-side up on a baking sheet. Toast the buns under the broiler, watching closely so they don't burn. Set the top halves aside and divide the chicken enchilada filling evenly among the bottom bun halves. Top with the remaining 1 cup cheese.

Broil until the cheese has melted and the tops look toasty. Remove from the oven and place the top of the bun on each sandwich.

Memphis-Style BBQ Chicken Tacos with Coleslaw

Serves 6 to 8

Barbecue styles vary widely across the country. In Memphis, they use a dry rub and sometimes follow that up with a mop sauce. Even if you don't know exactly what that means, it sounds good! This recipe is a play on Memphis-style dry rub, only we're serving up this quick 'cue in corn tortillas, topped with creamy coleslaw. The mild spiciness of the chicken pairs perfectly with the slightly sweet crunch of the slaw. This is Taco Tuesday with a Tennessee twist!

1½ teaspoons paprika, preferably smoked paprika (but regular is fine)

¼ teaspoon black pepper

1½ teaspoons light brown sugar

¼ teaspoon salt

⅛ teaspoon cayenne pepper

¼ teaspoon garlic powder

¼ teaspoon dry mustard

4 cups shredded cooked chicken

1½ tablespoons cider vinegar

FOR THE COLESLAW

1 (16-ounce) bag coleslaw mix

½ cup mayonnaise

2 tablespoons granulated sugar

1 tablespoon cider vinegar

Salt and black pepper

12 to 16 corn tortillas, for serving

In a small bowl, stir together the paprika, black pepper, brown sugar, salt, cayenne, garlic powder, and mustard. Put the chicken in a large microwave-safe bowl, sprinkle the spice mixture over the chicken, and toss to coat. Add the vinegar and stir. Microwave the chicken for 45 seconds to 1 minute, until hot.

For the coleslaw, in a large bowl, stir together the coleslaw mix, mayonnaise, granulated sugar, and vinegar, season with salt and black pepper, and stir again until well combined.

To serve, warm the tortillas in a dry skillet over medium heat. Place ¼ cup of the chicken in each tortilla and top with the coleslaw.

Rustic Italian Sausage Soup

Serves 6

Soup doesn't have to be an all-day cooking affair. This recipe takes just fifteen minutes and makes a hearty, warm meal that's perfect for fall and winter. It relies heavily on pantry ingredients, so chances are you'll have what you need on hand. The soup is fabulous with warm rolls and a green salad.

1 teaspoon olive oil

1 pound bulk mild Italian sausage

1 small onion, diced

1 garlic clove, crushed

1 (15-ounce) can butter beans with liquid

1 (15-ounce) can black beans, drained and rinsed

1 (15-ounce) can diced tomatoes

1 (15-ounce) can beef broth

1 teaspoon dried basil

2 cups coarsely chopped kale leaves

½ cup shaved or shredded Parmesan cheese (optional)

In a large soup pot, heat the olive oil over medium heat. Add the sausage, onion, and garlic and cook, breaking up the sausage with a wooden spoon as it cooks, until the sausage is browned. Add the beans, tomatoes with their juices, broth, basil, and kale. Cook the soup for 5 minutes, or until heated through.

Ladle into bowls and serve topped with the Parmesan, if desired.

Hawaiian Smoked Sausage and Pineapple over Rice

Serves 6

The simple sweet-and-sour sauce in this recipe is one of my go-to sauces. Here it teams up with smoked sausage, pineapple, bell peppers, and onions for one of my favorite fifteen-minute meals. To keep within that time frame, I usually serve this with jasmine rice because it cooks quicker than other long-grain rice varieties. You can have your *o'hana* (Hawaiian for "family") gathered around the table together in short order with this meal.

2 tablespoons olive oil

1 onion, chopped into 1½-inch pieces

2 bell peppers (any color), chopped into 1½-inch pieces

1 garlic clove, crushed

1 pound smoked sausage links, cut into ¼-inch-thick coins

1 (20-ounce) can pineapple chunks in juice, drained, juice reserved

6 tablespoons packed light brown sugar

6 tablespoons distilled white vinegar

¼ cup soy sauce

2 tablespoons cornstarch

3 cups cooked rice

In a large skillet, heat the oil over medium-high heat. Add the onion, bell peppers, and garlic. Cook until the onion is soft, about 5 minutes. Add the sausage and reduce the heat to medium.

In a small bowl, stir together the reserved pineapple juice, brown sugar, vinegar, soy sauce, and cornstarch until well combined.

Add the sauce to the skillet and stir in the pineapple chunks. Raise the heat to medium-high and cook for 2 to 3 minutes, until the sauce begins to bubble and thicken. Serve over the rice.

Cheese Ravioli with Summer Garden Vegetables

Serves 4 to 6

Let's talk for a minute about picky eaters. There's at least one in every family, and sometimes it's not one of the kids. My method of dealing with picky ones is to let them get used to seeing things on their plates that they've declared they don't like. I let them pick out the zucchini or tomatoes and eat the part they do like. I do ask that they try the offending food. Eventually, they get used to seeing it on the plate and watching others eat it. As it becomes familiar, they're more likely to try it. This meal is perfect for serving to a mixed group—the picky and the veggie lovers. Let the less adventurous skip over the good stuff and focus on the ravioli. Everyone else can enjoy platefuls of vegetable-topped pasta.

2 tablespoons olive oil

1 zucchini, chopped

1 red bell pepper, chopped

1 small onion, chopped

1 garlic clove, crushed

1 (15-ounce) can diced tomatoes, with their juices

½ teaspoon dried basil

½ teaspoon dried oregano

Salt and black pepper

1 (24-ounce) bag frozen cheese ravioli

Bring a large pot of water to a boil.

Meanwhile, in a large skillet, heat the oil over medium heat. Add the zucchini, bell pepper, onion, and garlic and cook for 5 to 7 minutes, until the onion is soft. Stir in the tomatoes, basil, and oregano and season with salt and black pepper. Reduce the heat to low and simmer.

While the sauce is simmering, add the ravioli to the boiling water and cook according to the package instructions. Drain the ravioli and add them to the pan with the sauce, gently stirring to coat. Serve immediately.

Eggs Run Through the Garden

Serves 6

The first time I heard the old diner lingo "run it through the garden," I was covering the lunch shift in the restaurant where I worked in high school. In addition to the cafeteria line, we also had a grill that served short-order burgers, eggs, and more. I still remember the sweet older man who ordered his hamburger and told me to "run it through the garden," meaning to add lettuce, tomato, pickles, and onion to his burger. This time we're giving eggs the same treatment by cooking them with a pile of onions, zucchini, bell peppers, tomatoes, and herb seasoning. Teach your kids some diner lingo while you whip up this quick dish. Maybe you can get a volunteer for dish duty if you ask them to be the "bubble dancer" (dishwasher)!

3 tablespoons olive oil

¼ cup diced onion

1 garlic clove, crushed

1 small zucchini, diced

1 red bell pepper, diced

1 cup grape tomatoes, halved

½ teaspoon dried oregano

½ teaspoon dried thyme

¼ teaspoon paprika

¼ teaspoon black pepper, plus more as needed

¼ teaspoon salt, plus more as needed

6 large eggs, beaten

In a large skillet, heat the oil over medium heat. Add the onion, garlic, zucchini, and bell pepper and cook for 3 to 5 minutes, until the onion is soft. Add the tomatoes and stir to combine.

In a small bowl, stir together the oregano, thyme, paprika, black pepper, and salt. Sprinkle the seasonings over the vegetables and stir to combine.

Season the beaten eggs with salt and black pepper, then pour them into the skillet with the vegetables. Cook, stirring gently, until the eggs are cooked to your liking, being careful not to overcook them.

Apple-Chicken Sausage and Broccoli Slaw Bowls with Garlic Dijon Honey Sauce

Serves 4

This recipe gets its speed from fully cooked apple-chicken sausages and bagged broccoli slaw picked up in the produce section. Stir together a simple homemade sauce, and you have a quick dinner that is full of veggies and flavor. You won't believe this was made in just fifteen minutes.

½ cup honey

2 tablespoons Dijon mustard

2 tablespoons soy sauce

Salt and black pepper

2 to 3 tablespoons olive oil

1 (12-ounce) package pre-cooked apple-chicken sausages, sliced into coins

3 garlic cloves, crushed

2 (12-ounce) packages broccoli slaw

1 Granny Smith apple, cored and sliced into thin matchsticks

In a small bowl, stir together the honey, mustard, and soy sauce, season with salt and pepper, and set aside.

In a large skillet, heat the olive oil over medium heat. Add the sausage slices and cook until browned on both sides, transferring the slices to a bowl once browned. Add the garlic, broccoli slaw, and apple to the skillet and cook for 3 to 5 minutes. Pour the sauce into the skillet and toss to coat the slaw. Cook for 2 to 4 minutes more.

Serve the broccoli slaw in bowls, topped with the sausage slices.

MY REFRIGERATOR IS EMPTY TONIGHT

—

I have to admit that I really don't like to grocery shop. If you enjoy wandering the aisles, you may wonder why I don't like it. For me it stems from a strong dislike of running errands of any kind. It feels like busywork, and if I can find a way to get out of it, I will! (All blessings and gratefulness for the person who came up with online grocery ordering!)

Because of my strong dislike of errand-running, I've become really good at pulling together a dinner by using what I've got in the house. Sometimes that's easier than others, but I'm up for the challenge of crafting a recipe from next to nothing if it means I can skip a trip to the store.

In this chapter, I've pulled together a few of my favorite pantry meals. These dishes are built around items you can keep stocked in your kitchen. Many of the ingredients are shelf-stable, others will last quite a while in the refrigerator, and the rest are things commonly found in a reasonably stocked (or even nearly empty) kitchen.

The next time you feel like Mother Hubbard, turn to this chapter to find your dinner recipe. Don't forget to substitute if you don't have the exact ingredient called for in the recipe. I've included lots of ideas for making substitutions, but let your imagination and the contents of your pantry dictate. No need for a trip to the grocery.

Mexican Rice and Bean Bowls

Serves 6

This has been a go-to recipe in my house for twenty years. (If that's not a sign a recipe's a keeper, I don't know what is!) It was given to me by a friend back when I had little babies, and if it outlasted that exhausting season in my life, I know it can stand up to anything. It's perfect for so many reasons: it's fast, healthy, inexpensive, and filling. Oh, and delicious, of course. It's also extremely adaptable—it is vegan if you leave out the cheese. You can even adjust it at the table if you have a whole gamut of palates to contend with; let each member of the family choose their variety of salsa and the spiciness of their hot sauce.

2 to 3 tablespoons olive oil

1 onion, chopped

1 garlic clove, crushed

1 tablespoon chili powder

1 teaspoon ground cumin

2 (15-ounce) cans dark red kidney beans, drained and rinsed

1 cup salsa

3 cups cooked brown or white rice

Cheddar cheese, shredded, for serving (optional)

Sour cream, for serving (optional)

Salsa or hot sauce, for serving (optional)

In a large skillet, heat the oil over medium heat. Add the onion and garlic and cook until the onion is soft, about 5 minutes. Add the chili powder, cumin, beans, and salsa and cook, stirring, for several minutes.

Serve over the rice and top with cheese, sour cream, and extra salsa or hot sauce, if desired.

Creamy Pesto and Sun-Dried Tomato Bow Ties

Serves 4 to 6

You may have to intentionally stock your pantry with these items, but that bit of foresight makes this meal perfect when you need to make dinner with food you have on hand. You can have this on the table in the time it takes to boil the pasta!

16 ounces bow-tie pasta (farfalle)

1 (8-ounce) jar oil-packed sun-dried tomatoes, drained and chopped into bite-size pieces

1 (8-ounce) jar prepared pesto

½ cup half-and-half, warmed

Bring a large pot of water to a boil. Add the pasta and cook according to the package directions until al dente. Drain the pasta and return it to the pot.

Add the tomatoes, pesto, and half-and-half and stir to combine. Serve on plates or in shallow bowls.

5 MEAL BUILDERS TO KEEP IN YOUR PANTRY

1. Canned Tomato Products

Crushed tomatoes can be the base for nearly any type of Italian sauce for pasta, pizza, and more. Diced tomatoes are much easier to keep on hand than fresh, and they go in all kinds of Mexican and Italian dishes. Other tomato products worth keeping in the pantry include tomato sauce, paste, and salsa.

2. Beans

Canned beans make for quick meals, but you may also want to have dried beans on hand. Dried beans can be cooked and frozen, then used just like canned beans in soups, casseroles, Tex Mex–style dishes, and much more.

3. Broth

Chicken, beef, and vegetable broths are essential pantry ingredients. Make your own and freeze it or use canned or boxed varieties. Use them for soups and stews or for cooking grains or pasta.

4. Aromatics: Onions and Garlic

Onions and garlic are both essential in many, many recipes. They add so much flavor to any dish but really bring out the best when you're pulling together a quick, easy meal.

5. Grains and Pasta

Rice, quinoa, couscous, and all shapes of pasta are great building blocks for meals. Top them with your protein of choice mixed with veggies. Let your imagination guide you!

High-Five Pasta

Serves 6

It's hard to beat a five-ingredient meal, especially when it involves bacon and cheese. You'll have no trouble at all pulling this dish together, even after a busy day when your pantry is mostly empty. I've included my favorite method for cooking bacon, too. This is so much easier than frying it in a pan, and as a bonus, the cleanup is a cinch. Get ready for high-fives from your family when you serve them this meal!

1 pound bacon

16 ounces bow-tie pasta (farfalle)

1 cup half-and-half, warmed

1 cup shredded Parmesan cheese

1 (14-ounce) can diced tomatoes, drained

Salt and black pepper

Bring a large pot of water to a boil.

Line two rimmed baking sheets with aluminum foil and arrange the bacon slices on the sheets in a single layer. Place the baking sheets in the cold oven, then turn the oven to 400°F. Bake for 15 to 18 minutes, until the bacon is crisp.

Meanwhile, add the pasta to the boiling water and cook according to the package directions until al dente. Drain the pasta and return it to the pot.

Remove the bacon from the oven and chop. Stir the bacon, half-and-half, Parmesan, and tomatoes into the pasta and season with salt and pepper. Serve immediately.

Break-in-Case-of-Emergency Pasta Sauce

Serves 6

Spaghetti is one of the most popular "when all else fails" dinners. We've all had evenings where heating sauce and boiling water for pasta was the most we could handle. Thank goodness for meals like this on evenings like that! With this simple recipe, you'll never need to turn to the jar again for great sauce. And I promise it's just as easy. I've added variations to suit your mood and the contents of your pantry. This sauce fits the bill as a quick weeknight dinner, but you'll feel comfortable serving it to company, especially if you add meatballs or Italian sausage.

2 tablespoons olive oil

1 small onion, diced

2 garlic cloves, crushed

1 (28-ounce) can crushed tomatoes

1½ teaspoons dried oregano

1 teaspoon dried basil

1 teaspoon dried thyme

⅛ teaspoon sugar

¼ cup grated Parmesan cheese

Salt and black pepper

Cooked pasta, for serving

In a large skillet, heat the oil over medium heat. Add the onion and garlic and cook for 5 to 7 minutes, until the onion is soft. Stir in the tomatoes, oregano, basil, thyme, sugar, and Parmesan. Season with salt and pepper. Reduce the heat to medium-low and cook until the sauce is bubbling and hot.

Serve the sauce over hot pasta.

VARIATIONS There are many variations to this recipe. Try adding ½ cup red wine to the pan after the onions and garlic are cooked. Let that reduce for 1 to 2 minutes before adding the other ingredients. Substitute two 15-ounce cans tomato sauce for the crushed tomatoes. Feel free to adjust the seasonings to suit your tastes, adding more or less or trying fresh herbs instead of dried. Make the sauce cheesier by adding a small amount of mozzarella or Provolone, or make it vegan by skipping the cheese.

Western Scramble Skillet

Serves 4 to 6

This is a great recipe to tuck away for when your pantry is looking empty. It lends itself to substitutions, making it perfect for using up the last little bits of this and that. Learn to trust yourself in changing up recipes to fit what you have in your kitchen. Eating at home quickly gets derailed when it involves last-minute trips to the grocery. In most cases, you can substitute something else and still have a delicious dinner. The version I've included here combines potatoes, bell peppers, onions, and ham. The eggs get scrambled, which is quicker and easier than making a traditional omelet. Cheese melts into everything, so you know it's a winner!

3 tablespoons olive oil

2 small potatoes, unpeeled, cut into cubes

1 small onion, chopped

½ red bell pepper, chopped

½ green bell pepper, chopped

1 cup cubed ham

6 large eggs, beaten

Salt and black pepper

4 slices Colby Jack cheese

In a large skillet, heat the oil over medium heat. Add the potatoes and onion and cook for 6 to 7 minutes, until the onion is soft. Add the bell peppers and cook, stirring occasionally, for 2 to 3 minutes more. Add the ham and cook for 4 to 5 minutes more, until the potatoes are tender.

Season the beaten eggs with salt and black pepper, then pour the eggs evenly over the top of the veggies and ham in the skillet. Gently stir until the eggs are cooked to your liking. Be careful not to overcook the eggs.

Remove the skillet from the heat and place the cheese slices over everything. Cover and allow the cheese to melt for 1 to 2 minutes. Serve.

VARIATION Use frozen hash browns instead of potatoes, bacon instead of ham, and/or different varieties of cheese.

Italian Tomato Soup with Pizza-Grilled Cheese Croutons

Serves 5 or 6

This may be the best tomato-soup-and-grilled-cheese meal I've ever had. My entire family loves it! I've given the classic combo a pizza-inspired spin, which takes it to a whole new level. Instead of serving the soup with sandwiches, we cut them into crisp cubes that are perfect for dunking into the bowl of hot soup. The croutons are stuffed with mozzarella cheese and pepperoni, like bite-size mini pizzas.

6 tablespoons (¾ stick) salted butter

1 small onion, diced

2 garlic cloves, crushed

2 tablespoons all-purpose flour

2 (15-ounce) cans tomato sauce

1 (14.5-ounce) can beef broth

1 teaspoon dried basil

1 teaspoon dried oregano

½ teaspoon sugar

Salt and black pepper

1 loaf Italian bread, sliced about
   ½ inch thick

8 ounces mozzarella cheese, sliced

6 ounces pepperoni

Preheat the broiler.

In a large pot, melt 2 tablespoons of the butter over medium heat. Add the onion and garlic and cook for 3 to 5 minutes, until the onion is soft. Whisk in the flour and cook, whisking continuously, for 1 minute. Whisk in the tomato sauce and broth. Stir in the basil, oregano, and sugar and season with salt and pepper. Reduce the heat to low and let the soup simmer while you make the sandwiches.

Use the remaining 4 tablespoons butter to butter 2 slices of bread per sandwich. Place half the bread slices buttered-side down on a baking sheet. On each, layer a slice of cheese, a few pepperoni, and another slice of cheese. Top each with a second slice of bread, buttered-side up. Broil until the bread is toasty. Flip the sandwiches and broil until the second side is toasty too. Remove from the oven and cut the sandwiches in bite-size cubes.

Serve the soup in bowls, topped with the croutons.

Elvis Breakfast for Dinner

Serves 6 to 8

Elvis Presley was famous for a lot of things, and one of those was his penchant for peanut butter, banana, and bacon sandwiches. That combo may sound a bit odd, but when you flip it from sandwiches to peanut butter pancakes topped with sliced bananas and crumbled bacon, it becomes amazing! The great thing about this meal is you can deconstruct it for picky kids. The bananas never have to touch the pancakes or the bacon, if you want to serve everything separately. But for those who want to be "all shook up," pile the bananas and bacon on top of the pancakes and drizzle maple syrup over everything!

2 tablespoons distilled white vinegar

2 cups milk, plus more if needed

1¾ cups all-purpose flour

1½ teaspoons baking powder

1 teaspoon baking soda

1 teaspoon salt

2 large eggs

1 cup peanut butter

4 tablespoons (½ stick) salted butter, melted and cooled

Vegetable oil, for greasing

1 pound bacon, cooked and crumbled

3 or 4 bananas, sliced into rounds

Maple syrup, for serving

Heat a griddle or skillet over medium-low heat (if using an electric griddle, set it to 375°F).

Stir the vinegar into the milk and set aside.

In a large bowl, combine the flour, baking powder, baking soda, and salt. In a separate bowl, whisk the eggs and peanut butter together. Whisk in the milk and melted butter. Fold the wet ingredients into the dry ingredients, stirring gently to combine. Avoid overstirring; the batter will be lumpy.

Oil the griddle or skillet. Drop ¼ cup of the batter onto the griddle and cook the pancakes for 2 to 3 minutes, watching for the tops of the pancakes to start bubbling. Flip and cook until golden brown on the second side. Transfer the pancakes to a large plate or platter and repeat with the remaining batter. If the batter becomes too thick as it sits, stir in a bit of milk to thin it.

Serve the pancakes topped with the bacon, sliced bananas, and maple syrup.

Curried Chickpeas

Serves 6

If you're looking for a new go-to recipe—one that uses only pantry ingredients and can be made in about fifteen minutes—look no further. Recipes like this are perfect for nights when you come home late and need dinner on the table quickly. Serve this simple curry over white or brown rice, couscous, or quinoa.

2 tablespoons olive oil

1 onion, chopped

1 garlic clove, crushed

2 (15-ounce) cans chickpeas, drained and rinsed

2 (15-ounce) cans mild diced tomatoes with green chiles, with their juices (see Notes)

2 tablespoons curry powder

10 ounces (1¼ cups) canned coconut milk (see Notes)

Salt

In a large skillet, heat the oil over medium heat. Add the onion and garlic and cook for about 5 minutes, until the onion is soft. Stir in the chickpeas, tomatoes with green chiles and the juices from the can, the curry powder, and the coconut milk. Season with salt. Cook for 5 to 10 minutes more, until heated through. Serve hot.

NOTES Increase the heat by using spicier diced tomatoes with green chiles, or turn down the heat by using plain diced tomatoes without chiles.

Any extra coconut milk can be used as part of the liquid for cooking the rice, couscous, or quinoa.

EVERYONE'S ON A DIFFERENT SCHEDULE TONIGHT

———

A few things are true when everyone in the family has a different schedule in the evening. One, they all still want to eat when they get home. Two, it's a bit more challenging to come up with something that will work. Three, your family members are going to want something simple, especially if they're fixing their own plates—too many sides or things to heat up, and they won't be happy.

The recipes in this chapter work well because they can be made ahead of time and kept warm in a slow cooker or reheated in the microwave. Sandwich and taco fillings are favorites of mine when I've got people eating on different schedules. I've also included a simple make-your-own-pizza bar.

I have to admit that I had teens, specifically teen boys, in mind when I chose many of these recipes. Even on nights when I've made dinner for them and they were home to eat it, teen boys often wander back into the kitchen for a second dinner around nine or ten o'clock.

Whether you're feeding first or second dinner to teens or adults, old or young, this chapter will make it as easy as counting to three.

The Simplest Sloppy Joes

Serves 10 to 12

Growing up, we called sloppy joes "Wimpies." I have no idea where that name came from, but I thought everyone called them that until I grew up and moved away from Richmond, Indiana! My best guess is that it's a reference to Wimpy, the character in the *Popeye* comic strip who was famous for eating hamburgers.

But whatever you call them, these are not a wimpy little meal. These overstuffed sandwiches can feed even the most ravenous teenage boys (although you may want to plan on two or three buns each for them!). The best part is that you can leave the pot ready to go on the stovetop or keep the meat warm in a slow cooker, then let your family serve themselves as they come in and out from practices or other activities. They're especially perfect for keeping you out of the path of the hangry pre-dinner teenager! As a bonus, the meat filling freezes well. If you have growing kids who like sandwiches for a snack, freeze individual servings in muffin tins or small freezer bags. A quick spin in the microwave will defrost and heat them.

2 pounds ground beef

1 onion, diced

2 garlic cloves, crushed

1 celery stalk, diced

1 red bell pepper, diced

1 (15-ounce) can tomato sauce

12 ounces chili sauce

1 tablespoon red wine vinegar

1 tablespoon Worcestershire sauce

2 tablespoons light brown sugar

Salt and black pepper

10 to 12 whole-wheat hamburger buns

In a large skillet, combine the ground beef, onion, and garlic and cook over medium heat for 5 to 10 minutes, until the beef is partially cooked. Add the celery and bell pepper and cook until the beef is well browned. Drain the mixture in a colander to remove excess grease, then return it to the pan. Add the tomato sauce, chili sauce, vinegar, Worcestershire, and brown sugar and season with salt and black pepper. Cook over medium heat until warmed through, about 5 minutes.

Pull apart the buns, top each half with meat, and serve.

Royal Feast Pizza Sloppy Joes

Serves 6

The best—I mean the absolute best-in-the-whole-world—pizza can be found at a pizza place in my hometown. They serve the Royal Feast pizza, which is loaded with pepperoni, sausage, peppers, onions, and more. I decided to give the Royal Feast treatment to sloppy joes. There's no reason a humble sandwich can't be loaded with all the good stuff too! This recipe is a crowd-pleaser and perfect for nights when everyone is eating at a different time.

½ cup diced onion

½ cup diced red bell pepper

½ cup diced green bell pepper

1 pound bulk mild Italian sausage

¼ cup diced pepperoni

1 (15-ounce) can tomato sauce

1 teaspoon garlic powder

1 teaspoon dried oregano

Salt and black pepper

6 sandwich buns

6 slices mozzarella cheese

In a large skillet, combine the onion, bell peppers, and sausage and cook over medium heat until the sausage is nearly cooked through. Add the pepperoni and cook for a few minutes more, until the sausage is done. Drain excess grease from the pan, if needed. Add the tomato sauce, garlic powder, and oregano and season with salt and black pepper. Stir to combine. Cook over medium heat until hot and bubbling.

Meanwhile, toast the buns. Serve the sloppy joe filling on the toasted buns, topped with the cheese.

Greek Turkey Tacos

Serves 6 to 8

If you're looking for a way to transform your traditional tacos, look no further! These have all the ease you need on Taco Tuesday (or any other day of the week), but the flavors will have you thinking of gyros. Pair these with a simple Greek salad for a complete meal in minutes. For a homemade Greek seasoning recipe, see the Easy Greek Soup recipe on page 89.

2 pounds ground turkey

3 tablespoons Homemade Greek Seasoning (page 89)

1 cucumber, peeled, seeded, and diced

1½ cups plain Greek yogurt

1 garlic clove, crushed

Salt and black pepper

12 to 16 (6-inch) flour tortillas

1 cup crumbled feta cheese

2 cups shredded lettuce

2 tomatoes, diced

¼ cup diced red onion

In a large skillet, brown the turkey over medium heat. Stir in the Greek seasoning.

Meanwhile, in a small bowl, stir together the cucumber, yogurt, and garlic and season with salt and pepper.

Serve the turkey in the tortillas, topped with the cucumber-yogurt sauce, feta, lettuce, tomato, and onion.

Make-Your-Own-Pizza Bar with Naan Bread Crusts

Naan breads make fantastic quick pizza crusts. Allow one or two mini naan per person, and let everyone top it to suit their tastes. This works great for a crowd or when everyone needs to eat at a different time. I've given you five ideas, but the possibilities are nearly endless. Each recipe on the following two pages yields 6 to 8 mini naan pizzas.

Pizza-Building Directions

Preheat the oven to 400°F. Line a baking sheet with aluminum foil or parchment paper.

Set the naan in a single layer on the prepared baking sheet. Spread some sauce over each naan. Add the toppings. Sprinkle or mound with the cheese, using as much or little as you like. Bake for 10 to 15 minutes, until the cheese is melted and beginning to brown. Serve hot.

ALFREDO SAUCE (MAKES ABOUT 3 CUPS)

4 tablespoons (½ stick) salted butter

1 to 3 tablespoons all-purpose flour

2 cups half-and-half

2 cups shredded Parmesan cheese

Salt and black pepper

In a 3-quart saucepan, melt the butter over medium heat. Whisk in 1 tablespoon flour and cook for 1 minute. Whisk in the half-and-half until the sauce is smooth. Cook, stirring often, for 2 to 3 minutes, or until the sauce begins to bubble. The sauce will thicken as it cools, but if you'd like a thicker sauce, add 1 to 2 more tablespoons of flour. Remove from the heat and stir in the Parmesan. Season with salt and pepper. Taste and adjust the seasoning as you like. The sauce can be used right away or stored in an airtight container in the refrigerator for several days.

CLASSIC RED SAUCE (MAKES ABOUT 2 CUPS)

1 (15-ounce) can crushed tomatoes

1 teaspoon red wine vinegar

½ teaspoon dried basil

¼ teaspoon dried oregano

¼ teaspoon garlic powder

Salt and black pepper

In a medium bowl, stir together the tomatoes, vinegar, basil, oregano, and garlic powder. Season with salt and pepper. Let stand for 15 to 30 minutes while you pull the other pizza ingredients together. No need to cook this one!

Alfredo Chicken Pizza

Alfredo Sauce (above)

1 to 2 cups shredded cooked chicken

Fresh tomatoes, sliced or chopped

Broccoli, cut into florets and steamed

Baby spinach

Bacon, cooked and crumbled

Red onion, thinly sliced or diced

3 to 4 cups shredded mozzarella cheese

Veggie Pizza with Classic Red Sauce or Alfredo Sauce

Classic Red Sauce or Alfredo Sauce (opposite)

Sliced tomatoes

Red onion, diced, raw or sautéed

Green, red, or yellow bell peppers, diced, raw or sautéed

Black and/or green olives, pitted and sliced

Baby spinach

Roasted red peppers

Sun-dried tomatoes, chopped

Mushrooms

Banana peppers, sliced

Fresh basil, chopped

3 to 4 cups shredded mozzarella cheese

Italian Sausage and Peppers with Classic Red Sauce

Classic Red Sauce (opposite)

1 pound bulk mild Italian sausage, browned

Red onion, diced and sautéed

Green, red, and yellow bell peppers, diced and sautéed

Black olives, pitted and sliced

Banana peppers, sliced

3 to 4 cups shredded mozzarella cheese

Pepperoni with Classic Red Sauce

Classic Red Sauce (opposite)

6 ounces pepperoni

Red and green bell pepper, diced

Red onion, thinly sliced or diced

Black olives, pitted and sliced

3 to 4 cups shredded mozzarella cheese

Barbecue Pizza

Your favorite barbecue sauce

1 to 2 cups shredded cooked chicken

1 to 2 cups diced cooked ham

Chopped pineapple

Red onion, thinly sliced or diced

Green bell pepper, thinly sliced or diced

Bacon, cooked and crumbled

3 to 4 cups shredded mozzarella cheese

1 to 2 cups shredded cheddar cheese

You-Won't-Miss-the-Meat Black Bean Burgers

Serves 8

My sons are currently in what I call "the age of meat," meaning they crave protein. This phase in boys starts as young as age ten and lasts a really long time. We haven't reached the end of it yet, and they are both in their twenties. If I try to serve a meatless meal, they will often growl a bit. But I'm happy to report that no growling or grumbling occurs when I serve these black bean burgers! You'll love them, too, because they are easy, full of flavor, and inexpensive. Leftover burgers can be reheated, sliced, and served in tortillas with taco fixings.

3 (15-ounce) cans black beans, rinsed and drained

2 cups panko bread crumbs

2 garlic cloves, crushed

½ medium onion, minced

1 large egg, beaten

1 teaspoon chili powder

½ teaspoon ground cumin

1 teaspoon salt

¼ teaspoon black pepper

2 to 3 tablespoons olive oil

8 slices cheddar cheese (optional)

8 hamburger buns

Toppings of your choice

Mash the beans in a large bowl using the back of a spoon until most are mashed but some are left whole or in pieces. Add the panko, garlic, onion, egg, chili powder, cumin, salt, and pepper and stir to combine. Pat the mixture into 8 burgers.

In a large skillet, heat the oil over medium heat. Add the burgers and cook for 5 minutes on each side. Top each burger with a slice of cheese, if desired, and let it melt, then remove them from the skillet.

Serve the burgers on the buns, with your choice of toppings.

I'M OUT OF THE HOUSE AND WON'T HAVE TIME TO COOK TONIGHT

———

Of all my kitchen appliances, I think I love my slow cooker best.
There's nothing like the feeling of satisfaction you get when you
load the slow cooker in the morning and know that no matter
what goes on during the day, no matter how busy things get, you'll
have dinner ready and waiting.

You may think about using a slow cooker only in cold weather,
but I love using mine year-round. It's perfect in the summer
because it doesn't heat up the kitchen. And you still get the same
benefit of having dinner waiting, whether it's after a day of work
or a day of fun.

For a few of the recipes in this chapter, I've also included
pressure cooker instructions. This appliance makes dinner
so easy. I choose the pressure cooker over the slow cooker on
days when I have a few minutes in the afternoon to pull dinner
together. I also really like using it on Sundays. I let the pot cook
under pressure while I'm getting dressed for church. By the time
we're ready to leave the house, it has switched over to the Keep
Warm setting, and the food is perfect when we get home.

Wild Card Chicken Soup

Serves 6 to 8

Soup is one of the best ways to turn miscellaneous scraps from the fridge or pantry into a satisfying, hands-off meal. This one is almost impossible to mess up, no matter what substitutions you make. Of course, it's wonderful when made according to the recipe, but feel free to alter it based on what you like, what you have on hand, and what you're in the mood for tonight. Here are a few ideas for changing it up: substitute whatever color bell pepper (or even other veggies) you like; try kidney beans or pinto beans; skip the rice for a lower-carb dinner; skip the chicken and double the beans to go vegetarian; warm yourself up by adding a heavy dose of hot sauce. Whatever you do, you'll spend the whole day thinking about coming home to this soup!

4 or 5 boneless, skinless chicken breasts

3 (15-ounce) cans chicken broth

1 (15-ounce) can diced tomatoes

1 (16-ounce) package frozen corn kernels

1 (15-ounce) can black beans, drained and rinsed

1 red bell pepper, chopped

1 onion, chopped

1½ teaspoons garlic powder

1½ teaspoons ground cumin

¼ cup Taco Seasoning (recipe follows)

½ cup uncooked white rice

1 cup shredded Monterey Jack cheese

Place the chicken breasts, broth, tomatoes with their juices, corn, beans, bell pepper, onion, garlic powder, cumin, and taco seasoning in a slow cooker. Cover and cook on High for 5 to 6 hours or on Low for 7 to 8 hours. Stir in the rice 30 minutes before serving.

Serve in bowls, topped with the shredded cheese.

TACO SEASONING

Makes about ½ cup (the equivalent of 2 store-bought seasoning packets)

3 tablespoons chili powder

1½ teaspoons garlic powder

¾ teaspoon onion powder

¾ teaspoon crushed red pepper flakes

¾ teaspoon dried oregano

1½ teaspoons paprika

4½ teaspoons ground cumin

1 tablespoon salt

1½ teaspoons black pepper

Combine all the ingredients in an airtight container and stir well. Cover and store in a cool, dark place for up to 6 months.

Slow-Simmered Root Vegetable Beef Stew

Serves 8

A big bowl of beef stew on a cool fall day or a cold, snowy evening warms you like snuggling under a cozy blanket in front of a fire. The slow cooker does most of the work for this simple stew. There is a bit of chopping, but even that can be comforting. Gather the veggies on the cutting board and let the sound of the knife slicing crisp carrots, potatoes, turnips, and parsnips remind you of all the blessings God has given. Gather your family and friends around the table to share the meal together. Steaming bowls of stew, hot buttered cornbread, and a house full of people you love is a lot to be thankful for.

2 pounds beef stew meat, cubed

1 onion, diced

2 or 3 garlic cloves, crushed

2 large potatoes, peeled and chopped

3 carrots, chopped

3 parsnips, peeled and chopped

1 turnip, peeled and chopped

1 (15-ounce) can tomato sauce

1 teaspoon dried thyme leaves

1 teaspoon kosher salt

1 teaspoon Worcestershire sauce

1 (32-ounce) container beef broth

Black pepper

3 tablespoons all-purpose flour

Place the beef, onion, garlic, potatoes, carrots, parsnips, turnip, tomato sauce, thyme, salt, Worcestershire, and broth in the slow cooker. Season with pepper. Cover and cook on High for 7 to 8 hours.

Meanwhile, in a jar with a tight-fitting lid, combine the flour and ¾ cup water, cover, and shake well. Pour the mixture into the stew to thicken it. Cook for 5 to 10 minutes more before serving.

Tacos al Pastor

Serves 6 to 8

How hot do you like it? It's really easy to turn up the heat on this recipe, but if your family likes to keep things cool, that's an option, too. The pork for tacos *al pastor* is traditionally cooked on a rotisserie. Pineapple and peppers are also used, giving the meat a sweet-and-spicy flavor. To keep things simple, this recipe uses the slow cooker. The result may not be traditional, but the fragrant smell will pull your family to the kitchen and have them wondering when dinner will be ready so they can dive in!

2 pounds pork loin or boneless roast

1 (7-ounce) can chipotle chiles in adobo sauce (optional; see Note)

1 onion, diced

1 garlic clove, crushed

1 (20-ounce) can pineapple tidbits in juice

1 teaspoon salt

¼ teaspoon black pepper

12 to 16 corn tortillas

2 cups shredded lettuce

½ cup chopped fresh cilantro

Lime wedges, for serving

Place the pork in a slow cooker.

Remove all the chiles from the can of chipotles and set aside. Spoon the sauce from the can into a medium bowl. Add the onion, garlic, pineapple tidbits with their juice, salt, and pepper.

Depending on how spicy you like your tacos, select 1 or 2 of the chipotle chiles (if you're using them). Slice the chile(s) lengthwise and scrape out the seeds. (The heat is found in the seeds, so removing them makes the chile less spicy.) Dice the chile(s) and add to the bowl with the onion mixture. Stir to combine. Pour the mixture into the slow cooker over the pork. Cover and cook on High for 5 to 6 hours or on Low for 7 to 8 hours. Shred the cooked meat with two forks.

Serve the pork in corn tortillas with lettuce and cilantro, and lime wedges on the side.

NOTE Extra chipotle chiles can be frozen for use in another recipe.

Elsa's Bahamian Chicken Souse

Serves 8

My husband often eats a packed lunch in the office. One day he commented on how great his coworker Elsa's lunch looked. She told him it was her version of her grandmother's Bahamian Chicken Souse. *Souse* means "drenched." Elsa shared her recipe with me, with the disclaimer that her grandmother would not approve of her version. Bahamian Chicken Souse seems to be one of those recipes, like chili, that has as many versions as there are cooks, and people stand by their family version as the only right one! I readily admit that I altered Elsa's version, mostly to simplify it. You know I love the slow cooker, so that's the cooking method I choose. If you're looking for a different spin on chicken soup, give this one a try! Pair it with Bahamian Johnny Cake (page 178).

4 pounds bone-in chicken pieces (legs, thighs, breasts, or wings)

2 teaspoons salt

½ teaspoon black pepper

1 teaspoon ground allspice

½ teaspoon garlic powder

3 celery stalks, chopped

1 onion, chopped

2 garlic cloves, crushed

3 medium potatoes, peeled and chopped

½ cup lemon juice

2 bay leaves

5 dashes of hot sauce (more or less, depending on how much heat you like)

Place the chicken in the slow cooker.

In a small bowl, stir together salt, pepper, allspice, and garlic powder. Sprinkle the seasonings over the chicken, tossing to coat each piece. Add the celery, onion, garlic, potatoes, lemon juice, bay leaves, hot sauce, and 4 cups water, arranging the vegetables over the chicken. Cover and cook on High for 6 to 8 hours. Remove the chicken from the pot and pull the meat from the bones; discard the bones. Return the meat to the soup and stir to combine. Discard the bay leaves and serve.

I Wish We Were in Paris Chicken Tarragon

Serves 6

Have you ever dreamed of taking a trip to Europe or some other faraway place? Jim and I had been dreaming of doing that ever since we were married. We saved airline miles and finally had enough for two tickets, but had just about determined that the trip wasn't going to happen. Then, during a snowstorm in February, we decided to go for it and planned the trip of a lifetime! We booked a trip to Paris for August, six months into the future. As happens so often in life, many things happened before the trip that made us rethink our decision. Several large items in our house stopped working and had to be replaced, including the heat pump and dishwasher. Jim had a bike wreck and suffered a severe concussion less than month before the trip. And France endured several terrorist attacks that summer. We had many reasons to cancel, but decided to go anyway. The trip turned out to be a great decision! Now we have so many memories of that week together, and our new motto is "Take the trip." It's easy to get entrenched in the mundane, talking ourselves out of the extravagant, but it's worth it to take those risks and really live life!

The French use tarragon quite a lot in cooking, and that's the herb I use here to flavor the chicken. This recipe makes use of the slow cooker, so it's not traditional at all, but it is achievable on a plain old Tuesday night, and it tastes special enough for a dinner with company. The onions in this dish have fantastic flavor!

1 tablespoon olive oil

2 large onions, sliced

1 tablespoon Dijon mustard

1 teaspoon dried tarragon

½ teaspoon salt, plus more as needed

¼ teaspoon black pepper, plus more as needed

2 to 3 pounds bone-in chicken breasts or thighs

Brush the inside of a slow-cooker insert with the oil. Place the onions in the bottom of the slow cooker. Add the mustard, tarragon, salt, and pepper and stir with a fork to combine. Place the chicken on top of the onions. Season the chicken with salt and pepper. Cover and cook on High for 5 to 6 hours or on Low for 7 to 8 hours. Serve with the onions alongside.

5-Minute Pesto-Rubbed Chicken

Serves 6

Any meal you can make that has a five-minute hands-on time *and* tastes like you've really spent hours cooking is a winner! This is one of those meals. You've got options when it comes to serving this dish, too. Pair it with buttered fettuccine or baked potatoes. Or try serving the meat on a sandwich along with sliced Provolone cheese, lettuce, and tomatoes. You might try making enough chicken to have it two nights in a row with both serving options.

1 tablespoon olive oil

1 large onion, sliced

2 pounds boneless, skinless chicken breasts

1 (8-ounce) jar prepared pesto

Brush the inside of a slow-cooker insert with the oil. Put the onions in the bottom of the slow cooker and place the chicken on top of the onions. Spoon the pesto over the chicken, using the back of the spoon to rub it into the chicken. Cover and cook on High for 4 to 5 hours or on Low for 6 to 7 hours.

Sea Salt Pork Chops and Potatoes with Gravy

Serves 6

If you're in need of some comfort food, this recipe will do the trick. The gravy is full of flavor and is wonderful served over the pork chops and potatoes. These traditional-style pork chops are really good served with colorful vegetables like sliced tomatoes and steamed broccoli. I've included both slow cooker and pressure cooker instructions, so you can choose the method that best fits your schedule.

2 pounds boneless pork chops

4 medium potatoes, scrubbed and quartered

1 onion, chopped

2 teaspoons rough sea salt or kosher salt

1 (15-ounce) can chicken broth

Black pepper

¼ cup all-purpose flour

Place the pork chops, potatoes, onion, salt, and broth in a slow cooker or pressure cooker and season with pepper. If using a slow cooker, cover and cook on High for 5 to 6 hours or on Low for 7 to 8 hours. If using a pressure cooker, seal the lid and set the cook time to 15 minutes, then quick-release the pressure or let the pot release naturally and switch to the Keep Warm setting.

About 15 minutes before you're ready to serve, remove the pork chops and potatoes from the slow cooker or pressure cooker and set them aside on a platter, covered with foil to keep warm.

In a jar with a tight-fitting lid, shake the flour and 6 tablespoons water together to combine; if the mixture seems too thick, add 1 to 2 tablespoons more water. While stirring, slowly pour the mixture into the broth left in the slow cooker or pressure cooker. Cook for 5 to 10 minutes more, until thickened.

Serve the gravy over the pork chops and potatoes.

Baked Maple Ham and Sweet Potatoes

Serves 6

You only need four ingredients for this recipe, which means it can be made on your busiest days. Let your slow cooker do the work, and come home to a dinner that tastes like a holiday meal. I like using real maple syrup as the sweetener, but you can also use honey or brown sugar, or reduce or skip the sweetener, if you'd rather.

2 pounds boneless ham

3 large sweet potatoes, peeled and quartered

4 tablespoons (½ stick) salted butter, cut into pats

¼ cup maple syrup

Salt and black pepper

Place the ham in a slow cooker. Pile the sweet potatoes on top of and around the ham. Scatter the butter pats over the ham and sweet potatoes and drizzle everything with the maple syrup. Season with salt and pepper. Cover and cook on High for 5 to 6 hours or on Low for 7 to 8 hours. Serve hot.

I DON'T HAVE TIME FOR DISHES TONIGHT

No one likes doing dishes. In this chapter, I've pulled together one-pot and one-pan recipes. Sheet-pan dinners, soups, and skillet meals all keep dishes to a minimum. I'm not going to lie to you, though—you will still have *some* dishes to do. Here are a few tricks to reduce them and make the task more pleasant.

- Baking sheets can be lined with parchment paper for easy cleanup. You can skip oiling the pan if it's lined.
- Start a sink of soapy water when you begin cooking. Wash as you go.
- Try to start dinner with an empty dishwasher (if you have one).
- Rinse dishes with hot water, because it makes drying easier.
- Rinse the suds out of the sink with cold water. Dish soap is formulated to foam in hot water, so the cold water kills the suds faster.
- Work with your spouse. Kids tend to clear out of the kitchen fast after dinner, leaving you to have a quiet conversation together.
- Put the kids to work and go read a book or watch a show.
- Use 100 percent cotton towels for drying, because they are more absorbent.
- Get a good scrubby that's safe on all types of pans.
- Put on some happy music.
- Listen to a podcast or audiobook.
- Call a friend and talk—we do this less and less these days, it seems.
- Think about three things you're grateful for.
- Pray for your family, friends, and other concerns on your heart.

NOTE Sheet-pan dinners require a very large baking pan if you're cooking for a family of six or more people. Inexpensive 14 × 20-inch rimmed baking sheets can be found at big box stores or online. If you don't have a large pan, you can always use two 9 × 13-inch baking sheets instead.

Foil-Baked Lemon Pepper Tilapia with Veggies

Serves 6 to 8

When I first started making these packets, I would make one for each person. Then one day I had a breakthrough: instead of cutting, crimping, and cleaning up six packets a night, I could do it all in one extra-big packet (see note below). So if you're making all the packets the same, go for the big one. But if you'd like to vary the contents according to the tastes of your family members, wrap individual packets. And if it's too hot to turn on the oven, try these on the grill. They'll be perfect grilled over medium heat for 15 to 20 minutes.

Cooking spray or oil mister
6 to 8 (4-ounce) tilapia fillets
¼ teaspoon lemon pepper seasoning
4 Roma (plum) tomatoes, sliced
3 or 4 green onions (scallions), sliced
Handful of fresh basil, chopped
3 to 4 tablespoons lemon juice

Preheat the oven to 450°F. Spread a large piece of foil on the counter (about 15 inches long). Spray with cooking spray or oil. Set the foil coated-side up on a rimmed baking sheet.

Place the tilapia in a single layer on the foil and sprinkle lightly with lemon pepper seasoning. Cover the tilapia with the tomatoes, green onions, basil, and lemon juice, and sprinkle with more lemon pepper seasoning. Cover with another 15-inch piece of foil and seal the edges of the foil so you end up with a loose packet. Bake for 20 minutes. Open the packet carefully to avoid being burned by the steam. Serve warm with the vegetables and any juices spooned over.

ALL-IS-NOT-LOST WORKAROUND If you're making one large packet or cooking on the grill, you'll need heavy-duty foil. But if you don't have that on hand, try doubling regular foil. For the individual packets, regular foil will work fine.

One-Sheet Autumn Pork Chops with Apples and Sweet Potatoes

Serves 4 to 6

Even if the leaves aren't turning shades of red and gold, this meal will give you a hint of beautiful autumn flavor. The ingredients are few, but the simple seasonings allow the taste of the pork, apples, and sweet potatoes to really shine through. A sprinkle of cinnamon stirs up hints of fall.

4 or 5 tablespoons olive oil

4 to 6 (1-inch-thick) boneless pork chops

Salt and black pepper

4 medium sweet potatoes, peeled and cubed

4 or 5 medium apples, peeled, cored, and cut into ½-inch-thick slices (see Note)

1 tablespoon salted butter, melted

¼ teaspoon ground cinnamon

Preheat the oven to 425°F. Grease a large baking sheet with 1 to 2 tablespoons of the oil.

Place the pork chops on one end of the prepared baking sheet and season them with salt and pepper.

In a large bowl, toss the sweet potatoes with the remaining 2 to 3 tablespoons olive oil and season with salt and pepper. Spread the sweet potatoes into an even layer on the baking sheet alongside the pork chops, leaving space for the apples (set the bowl aside—no need to wash it). Roast for 15 minutes.

Meanwhile, in the same bowl you used for the sweet potatoes, toss the apples with the melted butter and cinnamon. At the 15-minute mark, remove the baking sheet from the oven and add the apples. Return the pan to the oven and roast for 15 to 20 minutes more, until the pork chops are cooked through and the sweet potatoes tender.

NOTE Any type of apple will work for this recipe. I use whatever I have in the fruit bowl: Red Delicious, Golden Delicious, Fuji, Gala, etc.

Skillet Chicken Potpie
with Drop Biscuit Crust

Serves 6

Chicken potpie has a reputation for taking a long time to make. This skillet version proves it's possible to have homemade chicken potpie in short order. If you happen to have cooked chicken in the freezer, it will be even quicker. But no worries if you need to start with raw chicken. You're still only minutes from having dinner on the table.

1 tablespoon olive oil

1½ pounds boneless, skinless chicken, cut in bite-size pieces

Salt and black pepper

½ onion, diced

3 tablespoons salted butter, at room temperature

3 tablespoons all-purpose flour

1 cup chicken broth, plus ¼ to ½ cup more, if needed

¾ cup milk

1 (12-ounce) bag frozen peas and carrots

FOR THE BISCUITS

1 cup all-purpose flour

1 tablespoon baking powder

½ teaspoon salt

3 tablespoons salted butter

¾ cup milk

Preheat the oven to 400°F.

In a 12-inch ovenproof skillet, heat the oil over medium heat. Season the chicken with salt and pepper, add it to the skillet, and cook for 10 to 12 minutes, until it is cooked through. Transfer the chicken to a plate and set aside.

Add the onion to the skillet and cook for about 5 minutes, until soft. Add the butter and allow it to melt. Whisk in the flour to form a smooth paste. Cook for 1 minute. Whisk in the broth, followed by the milk. Cook until the sauce begins to thicken. Add the peas and carrots and return the chicken to the skillet. Season with salt and pepper. If the sauce seems too thick, add a little more broth to thin it a bit. It should be the consistency of very thick gravy. Remove the pan from the heat.

(recipe continues)

For the biscuits, in a large bowl, combine the flour, baking powder, and salt. Add 2 tablespoons of the butter and cut it into the flour with a fork or pastry blender until it forms soft crumbs. Stir in the milk until well combined.

Drop tablespoons of the dough on top of the potpie filling in the skillet. Transfer the pan to the oven and bake for 10 to 15 minutes.

Meanwhile, melt the remaining 1 tablespoon butter.

Remove the potpie from the oven and brush the biscuit topping with the melted butter. Return the pan to the oven for 1 to 2 minutes to brown the tops of the biscuits.

NOTE If you don't have a large ovenproof skillet, combine the filling ingredients in a casserole dish and then top and bake as directed.

Table Conversation Starters

What signature food would you like to be known for?

Would you like to be famous one day? Why or why not?

If you could be friends with a fictional book character, who would it be?

What's your favorite part of the day?

Who did you help today and how did you help them?

Who helped you today and how did they help?

What did you learn today? It doesn't have to be school related.

Which do you think is more important: music or visual arts?

What's one subject they don't teach in school that you wish they would?

Name a place in your hometown that you'd like to visit but never have. Make plans to go!

If you had out-of-town guests coming to visit, what would you take them to see in your town?

If you could instantly be good at one thing, what would it be?

Do you think it's good to be bored sometimes?

What's your favorite thing to do when you're bored?

What's one daring thing you'd like to try? It doesn't have to be daring for everyone, just daring for you.

If you could bump into a famous person during the day tomorrow, who would you choose?

Would you ever consider living in an historic time period (if time travel were possible)? Which one and why?

Do you think it's better to binge-watch a TV show or wait on new episodes to be released?

Which do you like more: starting things or finishing them?

How much time do you think people should spend on the Internet each day?

What's your favorite thing to do online?

One-Sheet Asian Salmon, Snap Peas, and Potatoes

Serves 6

You've got options with this meal. Actually, you have options with just about every meal in this book, but sheet pan dinners make it so simple to substitute ingredients. Just about anything works on a sheet pan, so let your imagination and the contents of your refrigerator be your guide. I've used white potatoes here, but sweet potatoes pair really well with salmon. Snap peas add a touch of green to the dish, but feel free to use green beans or Brussels sprouts or broccoli. It's your dinner—make it your own!

1 to 3 tablespoons olive oil

3 large potatoes, peeled and chopped into 1-inch pieces

Kosher salt and black pepper

¼ cup soy sauce

1 garlic clove, crushed

½ teaspoon sesame oil

12 ounces fresh or frozen sugar snap peas

6 salmon fillets

Preheat the oven to 400°F. Grease a large baking sheet with several teaspoons of the olive oil.

In a large bowl, drizzle 1 tablespoon or more of the olive oil over the potatoes. Season with salt and pepper and toss to coat the potatoes with the oil. Spread the potatoes over one end of the prepared baking sheet and roast for 10 minutes.

Meanwhile, in a small bowl, stir together the soy sauce, garlic, and sesame oil and season with pepper.

In the same bowl you used for the potatoes, drizzle the snap peas with the remaining oil and season with salt and ¼ teaspoon pepper. Pull the baking sheet from the oven and place the salmon fillets on the pan. Pour the soy sauce mixture over the salmon. Add the snap peas to the pan as well. Bake for 15 to 20 minutes, until the salmon flakes easily with a fork and the potatoes are tender.

NOTE Small vegetables like green beans and snap peas can be added to the pan while still frozen. They thaw and roast quickly, making them convenient for easy dinners.

One-Sheet Chili-Honey-Glazed Pork Chops, Butternut Squash, and Green Beans

Serves 4 to 6

This dish is not spicy at all, despite having "chili" in the name. The combination is a bit unusual, but chili powder and honey come together for a sweet-savory glaze that will have your family asking for more! If you do like spicy foods, it's easy to turn up the heat by using chipotle chili powder instead of the regular variety. Or add a dash or three of hot sauce to the glaze.

Vegetable oil, for greasing

1 tablespoon salted butter, melted

1 tablespoon honey

¾ teaspoon chili powder

¼ teaspoon salt, plus more as needed

4 to 6 (1-inch-thick) boneless pork chops

2 tablespoons olive oil

1 large butternut squash, peeled, seeded, and cut into ½-inch cubes

Black pepper

1 pound frozen or fresh green beans

Preheat the oven to 425°F. Grease a large rimmed baking sheet with oil.

In a small bowl, stir together the melted butter, honey, chili powder, and salt. Place the pork chops on one section of the baking sheet and spread the honey-chili glaze evenly over each chop.

In a large bowl, drizzle 1 tablespoon of the olive oil over the butternut squash cubes. Season with salt and pepper and toss to coat with the oil. Spread the squash in a single layer next to the chops on the baking sheet, leaving space for the green beans. Bake for 15 minutes.

Meanwhile, in the same bowl you used for the squash, drizzle the green beans with the remaining 1 tablespoon olive oil and season with salt and pepper, tossing to coat with the oil.

At the 15-minute mark, pull the pan from the oven and add the green beans. Bake for 10 to 15 minutes more, until the pork chops are cooked through and the squash is tender.

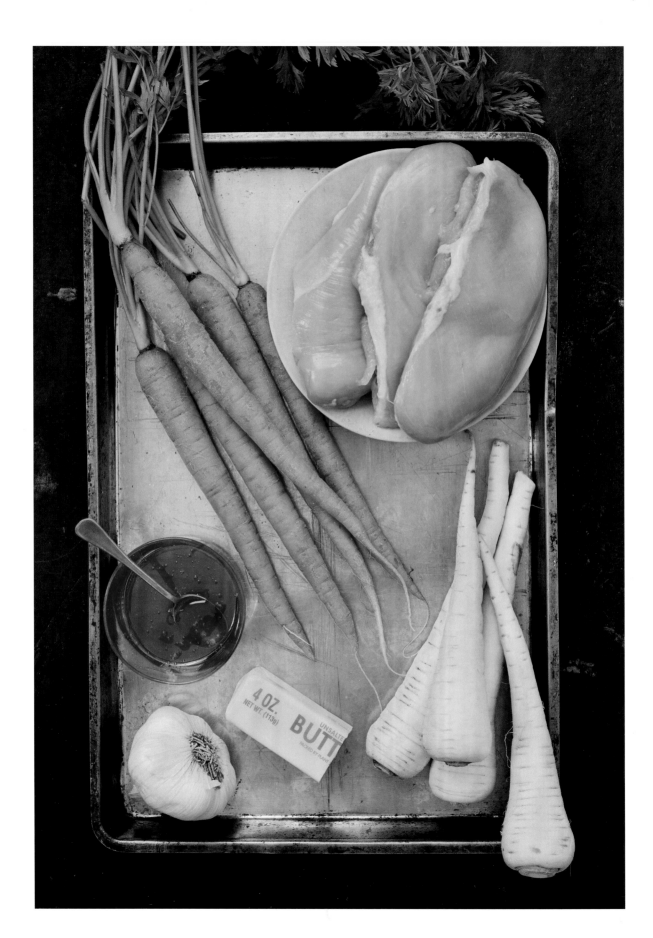

One-Sheet Roasted Garlic Chicken with Honey-Butter Carrots and Parsnips

Serves 6

If you're trying to convince the picky eaters in your life to expand their palates and add variety to the types of vegetables they're willing to eat, this is a great meal to try. Parsnips aren't too far from carrots in flavor. In fact, when I'm introducing them to kids (or grown-up picky eaters), I say they're like white carrots. In this sheet pan meal, the carrots and parsnips are tossed in honey butter and roasted. They aren't mushy, and their slightly sweet flavor will win over the biggest skeptics. Garlic-butter chicken shares the pan, and the flavors contrast wonderfully with the veggies. This meal will make the favorites list of the whole family.

1 tablespoon olive oil

2 pounds boneless, skinless chicken breasts

3 garlic cloves: 1 halved, 2 crushed

5 tablespoons salted butter, melted

Salt and black pepper

1 pound carrots, peeled and chopped

1 pound parsnips, peeled and chopped

2 tablespoons honey

Preheat the oven to 425°F. Grease a large rimmed baking sheet with the oil.

Place the chicken breasts on one end of the baking sheet. Rub each chicken breast with one of the garlic halves. Discard the garlic halves.

In a small bowl, stir together 2 tablespoons of the melted butter and the crushed garlic cloves. Season with salt and pepper. Brush the garlic butter over the chicken. Bake for 5 to 10 minutes.

Meanwhile, place the carrots and parsnips in a large bowl. In a small bowl, stir together the remaining 3 tablespoons melted butter, the honey, and a little salt and pepper. Pour the honey butter over the vegetables and toss to coat.

Remove the baking sheet from the oven and add the vegetables to the pan. Bake for 20 to 25 minutes, until the chicken is cooked through and the vegetables are tender.

One-Pot Sausage, Corn, and Red Pepper Chowder with Parmesan

Serves 6

I love taking a favorite recipe and giving it a new spin. It's the best of the familiar and new at the same time, like seeing a musical for the first time when you already know all the songs. Or reading a new book in a beloved series. This soup is just like that! Corn chowder is one of my family's favorite soups. For this version, I added Italian sausage and red bell peppers and topped each steaming bowl with Parmesan cheese. This is a hearty soup, perfect for hungry appetites on a cold day. Cook a big pot of this to follow a family leaf-raking session or a sledding party. Don't forget to add hot bread and a green salad!

1 medium onion, diced

1 pound bulk mild Italian sausage

2 tablespoons salted butter

3 tablespoons all-purpose flour

2 cups chopped peeled potatoes

1 red bell pepper, diced

1 (32-ounce) container chicken broth

1 bay leaf

1 cup frozen corn kernels

1 cup half-and-half

Salt and black pepper

½ cup shaved or shredded Parmesan cheese

In a large soup pot, brown the onion and sausage over medium heat. When the sausage is cooked, add the butter and allow it to melt. Stir in the flour and cook, stirring, for 1 minute. Add the potatoes, bell pepper, broth, and bay leaf. Bring to a boil and cook until the potatoes are tender, 10 to 15 minutes. Stir in the corn and half-and-half. Cook the soup for 5 to 10 minutes more, being careful not to let the soup boil. Season the soup with salt and black pepper. Discard the bay leaf.

Serve the soup in bowls, topped with the Parmesan.

Skillet Swiss Frittata with Spinach and Tomatoes

Serves 4 to 6

Frittatas are great for weeknight dinners or weekend brunch. This simple recipe is colorful, flavorful, and packed with veggies. I served this to my family after the kids finished soccer practice, and we had no leftovers. This recipe is on regular rotation in our house! You will need a large ovenproof skillet, but if you don't have one, no worries. Just pour the ingredients into a large, deep-dish pie pan instead.

2 tablespoons olive oil

1 tablespoon salted butter

½ onion, diced (about ½ cup)

2 cups baby spinach

¾ cup grape tomatoes, halved

½ cup milk

½ teaspoon kosher salt

¼ teaspoon black pepper

8 large eggs, beaten

1 cup shredded Swiss cheese

Preheat the oven to 350°F.

In a 10-inch skillet, heat the oil and butter over medium heat. Add the onion and cook for 2 to 3 minutes, until soft. Reduce the heat to medium-low and add the spinach. Cook, stirring gently, until the spinach wilts. Add the tomatoes and cook for 1 to 2 minutes.

Stir the milk, salt, and pepper into the beaten eggs. Pour the eggs into the skillet and stir to combine with the vegetables. Add the cheese, stirring gently to distribute the cheese through the eggs. Place the skillet in the oven and bake for 15 to 20 minutes, until the eggs are set.

I WANT TO COOK FOR TONIGHT *AND* TOMORROW NIGHT

—

If you or your family aren't thrilled with leftovers, this chapter will show you there's actually a lot to love about them. First, cooking once and eating twice is pretty hard to beat! It takes almost no extra work to make enough for two (or more) meals.

The main part of all these recipes can be frozen. That means you don't need to eat them the next day, or even the same week. Save the second serving suggestion for a later date, and your family will think they're eating a whole new meal!

There are a lot of ways to use all these recipes, in addition to the serving ideas I've given you. Let your imagination guide you to new variations. When you find one you like, jot a note next to the recipe so you'll remember.

Slow-Cooker African Pulled Beef

Makes 8 to 10 servings, to serve 4 or 5 people each night

Believe it or not, I developed this recipe based on a recipe I've only heard about, never eaten! You see, I'm a huge Disney fan, and I follow several blogs and Instagram accounts that cover Disney World food. Several years ago, one of the restaurants in Animal Kingdom rolled out a new dish of pulled beef, seasoned with African spices and served in pita bread. It got rave reviews online, and I eventually used that menu description to create this recipe. I'm sure it's nothing like the Disney version, and sadly, we'll never know because they no longer serve it! This version, however, has also gotten rave reviews from my family, even the picky eaters. Despite the jalapeño, it's not too spicy, but it's a nice change of pace from your typical barbecue beef.

1 (2- to 3-pound) beef chuck roast

3 to 5 garlic cloves: 1 halved, the others crushed

1 teaspoon ground cumin

½ teaspoon cayenne pepper

¼ teaspoon ground allspice

1 onion, diced

1 jalapeño, seeded and diced

1 (15-ounce) can diced tomatoes

Rub the roast thoroughly with the garlic halves. Place the roast, garlic halves, and crushed garlic in a slow cooker. Sprinkle with the cumin, cayenne, allspice, onion, and jalapeño. Pour the diced tomatoes over everything. Cover and cook on High for 5 to 6 hours or on Low for 7 to 8 hours.

Remove the meat from the slow cooker and shred it with two forks. Return the meat to the slow cooker and stir to combine with the juices. Ready to serve using one of the recipes on the next page. Use half tonight and refrigerate half for tomorrow night.

Tonight: Pulled Beef and Greek Yogurt Pitas

Serves 4 or 5

10 ounces plain Greek yogurt

1 large cucumber, peeled and diced

½ teaspoon dried mint

4 or 5 servings Slow-Cooker African Pulled Beef, warmed

4 or 5 pita breads

In a small bowl, stir together the yogurt, cucumber, and mint. Serve the beef in the pitas, topped with the yogurt sauce.

Tomorrow: Beefy Baked Sweet Potatoes with Crumbled Feta

Serves 4 or 5

4 or 5 large sweet potatoes, scrubbed

4 or 5 servings Slow-Cooker African Pulled Beef, warmed

4 ounces feta cheese, crumbled

1 bunch fresh flat-leaf parsley or cilantro, chopped

Preheat the oven to 400°F. Line a baking sheet with aluminum foil.

Poke each sweet potato several times with a sharp knife and place them on the prepared pan. Cover the pan tightly with another sheet of foil. Bake for 1 hour, or until the potatoes are tender in the center.

To serve, slice each potato down the middle lengthwise and fluff the inside. Top with the beef, feta, and parsley or cilantro.

It's Greek to Me

Full confession—I've never eaten a Greek soup and don't know what it would really be like. I do know that this twist on taco soup made my whole family happy. Instead of taco seasoning, I used homemade Greek seasoning. I also changed the black beans to great northern beans, added sliced black olives, and topped our bowls with crumbled feta. The second night turns the soup into Greek nachos, topped with cucumber, red onion, and feta and drizzled with tzatziki sauce.

Tonight: Easy Greek Soup

Serves 6, with leftovers for tomorrow night's Greek Nachos

2 pounds ground beef

1 onion, diced

1 garlic clove, crushed

2 (15-ounce) cans diced tomatoes

2 (2.5-ounce) cans sliced black olives, drained

2 (15-ounce) cans great northern beans, drained and rinsed

¼ cup Homemade Greek Seasoning (recipe follows)

2 (15-ounce) cans beef broth

¼ cup crumbled feta cheese

In a large soup pot, combine the ground beef, onion, and garlic in a large soup pot and cook until the beef is browned. Drain any excess grease and return the mixture to the pot. Stir in the tomatoes, olives, beans, Greek seasoning, and broth. Heat over medium heat for 15 to 20 minutes, until hot.

Serve topped with the crumbled feta.

HOMEMADE GREEK SEASONING

Makes about ¼ cup

2 teaspoons salt

2 teaspoons garlic powder

2 teaspoons dried basil

2 teaspoons ground oregano

1 teaspoon black pepper

1 teaspoon dried rosemary

1 teaspoon dried dill

1 teaspoon dried marjoram

1 teaspoon cornstarch

½ teaspoon ground cinnamon

½ teaspoon dried thyme

¼ teaspoon ground nutmeg

Combine all the ingredients in a mortar and use the pestle to crush and combine them. (Alternatively, use a small bowl and crush the spices with the bowl of a ladle.) Transfer to an airtight container and store in a cool, dark place for up to 6 months.

Tomorrow: Greek Nachos

Serves 6

6 to 8 pita breads, cut in triangles

1 tablespoon olive oil

1 (5-ounce) container plain Greek yogurt

1 teaspoon lemon juice

1 teaspoon dried dill

1 garlic clove, crushed

Salt and black pepper

3 to 4 cups Easy Greek Soup, warmed

1 cup diced cucumber

¼ cup diced red onion

¼ cup crumbled feta cheese

Preheat the broiler.

Brush the pita triangles with the oil. Place in a single layer on a baking sheet and broil for 2 to 5 minutes, until toasted.

Meanwhile, in a small bowl, stir together the yogurt, lemon juice, dill, and garlic and season with salt and pepper. Set the tzatziki sauce aside.

Remove the pita triangles from the oven. Using a slotted spoon, spread the meaty part of the soup over the pita triangles. Place under the broiler for 2 to 3 minutes more. Remove from the oven and scatter the cucumber, red onion, and feta over the top. Drizzle with the tzatziki sauce and serve.

Turkey Meat Loaf, Two Ways

It is easy to double your efforts when making meat loaf: one loaf to serve and one to freeze for later. Serve the first as a traditional meat loaf dinner with potatoes and a green vegetable. The second gets dished up as the best meat loaf sandwich you'll ever eat! Topped with two different sauces—Sweet Sauce and Cheater Aïoli—sautéed onions, and Swiss cheese on toasted buns, this sandwich is amazing. And trust me, you will want both of those sauces on your sandwich. It's so good!

Tonight: Classic American Turkey Meat Loaf

Makes 2 loaves, to serve 6 to 8 people each night

3 pounds ground turkey

1 small onion, diced

2 garlic cloves, crushed

1 (8-ounce) can tomato sauce

1 tablespoon Worcestershire sauce

1½ cups bread crumbs

2 large eggs

1½ teaspoons salt

½ teaspoon black pepper

2 teaspoons parsley flakes

1 teaspoon light brown sugar

Preheat the oven to 350°F. Line two 9 × 13-inch baking pans with foil.

In a large bowl or in the bowl of a stand mixer fitted with the paddle attachment, combine the turkey, onion, garlic, half the tomato sauce, the Worcestershire, bread crumbs, eggs, salt, pepper, and parsley flakes. Using your hands or with the mixer running on low, work the ingredients together just until combined; do not overwork or the meat loaf will be tough.

Form the mixture into two loaves and place one in each of the prepared pans. Cover with foil and bake for 1½ hours.

Meanwhile, stir the brown sugar into the remaining tomato sauce.

Remove the loaves from the oven, remove the foil, and top each loaf with the tomato sauce. Bake, uncovered, for 5 to 10 minutes more.

Serve one loaf tonight and refrigerate the other for tomorrow's meal.

Tomorrow: Turkey Meat Loaf Subs with Sweet Sauce and Cheater Aïoli

Serves 6 to 8

1 Classic American Turkey Meat Loaf

2 tablespoons olive oil

1 onion, thinly sliced

6 to 8 hoagie buns

6 to 8 slices Swiss cheese

Sweet Sauce (recipe follows)

Cheater Aïoli (recipe follows)

Preheat the broiler.

Slice the meat loaf.

In a small skillet, heat the oil over medium heat. Add the onion and cook, stirring, for 10 to 15 minutes, until browned.

Split the hoagie buns and place them on a baking sheet. Toast them under the broiler for 1 to 3 minutes. Pull the buns from the oven, top each with a slice of meat loaf, some onions, and a slice of Swiss cheese. Place the sandwiches back under the broiler to melt the cheese.

Remove from the oven and spread some of each sauce on the top buns. Close the sandwiches and dig in!

SWEET SAUCE

Makes about ¼ cup

¼ cup ketchup

2 teaspoons light brown sugar

Pinch of ground nutmeg

In a small bowl, stir together the ketchup, brown sugar, and nutmeg.

CHEATER AÏOLI

Makes about ¼ cup

¼ cup mayonnaise

½ teaspoon lemon juice

1 small garlic clove, crushed

Salt and black pepper

In a small bowl, stir together the mayonnaise, lemon juice, and garlic and season with salt and pepper.

Double Chicken Dinner

Please don't be intimidated by cooking a whole chicken. It's very easy, you get a lot of meat for your effort, and it's bargain-friendly, too. Rubbing the chicken with Dijon mustard, salt, and pepper gives a lot of flavor and keeps the meat moist. I've included three different cooking methods—choose the one that fits your day best. The slow cooker can be started in the morning and then you're free the rest of the day. Use the pressure cooker if you have time in the late afternoon to pull dinner together. The oven is nice when it's cold outside and you're home to cook.

The Dijon Pear Chicken Salad is a fresh take on a classic recipe. The pears add a sweetness that complements the chicken really well. I love this one for a make-ahead dinner or packable lunch.

Tonight: Dijon Chicken in the Slow Cooker, Pressure Cooker, or Oven

Serves 4 to 6, with leftovers for tomorrow night

1 (5- to 6-pound) whole chicken
1 tablespoon Dijon mustard
Salt and black pepper

Remove any giblets from inside the chicken and discard. Rub the mustard all over the outside of the chicken. Season with salt and pepper. Place the chicken in a slow cooker, pressure cooker, or baking dish.

Slow Cooker

Cover and cook on High for 5 to 6 hours or on Low for 7 to 8 hours.

Pressure Cooker

Pour 2 cups water around the chicken in the bottom of the pot. Seal the lid and set the cook time to 30 minutes. After cooking is complete, quick-release the pressure.

Oven

Preheat the oven to 350°F. Bake the chicken, uncovered, for 1½ to 2 hours, until the juices run clear when the meat is pierced with a knife.

(recipe continues)

Remove the cooked chicken from the slow cooker, pressure cooker, or oven and carve the meat from the bones. Set aside 2 cups of chopped cooked chicken for tomorrow night's dinner.

Serve the chicken with your choice of vegetables, salad, or rolls. Try the Power Chopped Salad (page 176) and Best-Ever Roasted Sweet Potatoes with Ginger, Cinnamon, and Thyme (page 187).

Tomorrow: Dijon Pear Chicken Salad

Serves 4 or 5

2 cups chopped Dijon Chicken

2 celery stalks, chopped

1 pear, peeled, cored, and chopped

⅓ cup chopped pecans

½ cup mayonnaise

½ teaspoon Dijon mustard

Salt and black pepper

4 to 5 cups spinach or lettuce leaves

In a large bowl, combine the chicken, celery, pear, and pecans. In a separate small bowl, stir together the mayonnaise and mustard and season with salt and pepper. Add the mayonnaise mixture to the bowl with the chicken and stir to coat everything well.

Serve the chicken salad over spinach or lettuce.

Garlicky Pulled Pork

Makes 8 to 10 servings, to serve 4 or 5 people each night

There are a number of good reasons to make this recipe for pulled pork, including the fact that it's freezable. Having cooked pork in the freezer makes future meals so easy. It's versatile, too. Pulled Pork Cuban Sliders are little sandwiches that pack a big flavor punch. I'll Do It Tamale is a cheater's way to make an easy tamale casserole. You can also turn the meat into barbecue sandwiches by stirring your favorite barbecue sauce into the meat. Choose your cooking method—use either a slow cooker or a pressure cooker. Both are easy!

1 (3½- to 4-pound) boneless pork roast

5 garlic cloves, crushed

1 teaspoon kosher salt

½ teaspoon black pepper

Slow Cooker

Place the pork roast in the slow cooker. Pour in ½ cup water. Put the garlic, salt, and pepper on the roast. Cover and cook on High for 5 to 6 hours or on Low for 7 to 8 hours.

Pressure Cooker

Place the pork roast in the pot. Pour in 2 cups water and top the roast with the garlic, salt, and pepper. Seal the lid and set the cook time to 60 minutes. Quick-release the pressure.

Remove the lid and take the meat from the slow cooker or pressure cooker. Shred the meat with two forks. Serve using one of the recipes that follow.

Tonight: Pulled Pork Cuban Sliders

Serves 4 or 5

2 to 3 cups Garlicky Pulled Pork, warmed

8 to 10 slider buns

6 ounces deli sliced ham

8 to 10 slices Swiss cheese

¼ cup dill pickle slices

2 tablespoons yellow mustard

Preheat the broiler.

Place a small amount of pulled pork on each bun. Top with several slices of ham and a slice of Swiss cheese. Set the sliders on a baking sheet and broil to melt the cheese.

Remove from the oven and top each slider with the pickles and mustard.

Tomorrow: I'll Do It Tamale

Serves 4 or 5

Cooking spray

1 (15-ounce) can tomato sauce

2 teaspoons chili powder

½ teaspoon ground cumin

½ teaspoon garlic powder

Salt

3 cups Garlicky Pulled Pork

½ cup cornmeal

¼ cup all-purpose flour

2 teaspoons baking powder

1 large egg

½ cup milk

Preheat the oven to 425°F. Spray a 2-quart casserole dish with cooking spray.

In a small bowl, stir together the tomato sauce, chili powder, cumin, and garlic powder and season with salt. Place the pork in the prepared casserole dish. Pour the tomato sauce mixture over the pork and stir to combine.

In a medium bowl, stir together the cornmeal, flour, baking powder, egg, and milk to make a batter. Pour the batter evenly over the pork. Bake for 20 minutes, until the cornbread is golden brown.

Beanless Firehouse Chili

Makes 8 to 10 servings, to serve 4 or 5 people each night

I withheld the beans from this chili because it's destined for ladling over my favorite macaroni and cheese and layering on nachos. I think those meals are best without the beans getting in the way of the other elements. However, it's your dinner, so make it the way you like! Feel free to add a can or two of kidney beans. Legumes or no legumes, this chili is so simple and quick to make. You can freeze any extra, which makes for a quick meal on another night. Just thaw, reheat, and try out the "Tomorrow" serving suggestion of Chili Waffle Fry Nachos.

2 pounds ground beef

1 large onion, diced

3 garlic cloves, crushed

2 (15-ounce) cans diced tomatoes

2 (15-ounce) cans tomato sauce

6 to 8 tablespoons chili powder (adjust to your family's taste)

1 teaspoon salt

½ teaspoon black pepper

In a large skillet or pot, combine the ground beef, onion, and garlic and cook over medium heat until the meat is browned and cooked through. Add the diced tomatoes with their juices, tomato sauce, chili powder, salt, and pepper. Cook over medium heat until hot and bubbling.

Tonight: Chili Waffle Fry Nachos

Serves 4 or 5

1 (24-ounce) bag frozen waffle fries

4 or 5 servings Beanless Firehouse Chili, reheated

2 cups shredded cheddar cheese

1 cup shredded lettuce

1 tomato, diced

¼ cup sour cream

Preheat the oven to 425°F.

Place the frozen waffle fries in a single layer on a large rimmed baking sheet. Bake for 20 minutes, then switch the oven to broil and broil the fries for 2 to 5 minutes, watching closely to make sure they don't burn. You want them browned and crisp on the edges, but not burnt. Pull the fries from the oven and spoon the chili over the top. Spread the cheese over all, pop the baking sheet back in the oven, and broil for 1 to 3 minutes. Watch closely and pull out the pan when the cheese has melted.

Serve topped with the lettuce, diced tomato, and sour cream.

Tomorrow: One-Pot Chili Mac and Cheese

Serves 4 or 5

8 ounces dry macaroni

½ teaspoon salt

¾ cup milk, warmed

¾ cup half-and-half, warmed

½ teaspoon dry mustard

1 cup shredded cheddar cheese

1 cup shredded Monterey Jack cheese

4 or 5 servings Beanless Firehouse Chili, warmed

Stovetop

Fill a 3-quart pot with water and bring to a boil. Add the macaroni and salt and cook for 10 minutes, until the macaroni is al dente. Drain the macaroni, leaving it a little wet, and return it to the pot. Add the milk, half-and-half, dry mustard, and both cheeses. Cook over low heat, stirring continuously, until the cheeses melt.

Pressure Cooker

In a pressure cooker, stir together the uncooked macaroni, salt, dry mustard, and 2 cups water. Seal the lid and set the cook time to 4 minutes. Quick-release the pressure, then remove the lid. Stir in the milk, half-and-half, and both cheeses. Set the pot to the Sauté setting. Cook, stirring frequently, until the cheeses have melted.

Serve in bowls, topped with the chili.

NOTE The pressure cooker version is my favorite way to make macaroni and cheese, but the stovetop works if you don't own a pressure cooker.

Bolognese Sauce for a Crowd

Makes 12 to 16 servings, to serve 6 to 8 people each night

This hearty pasta sauce makes enough to serve a crowd or to stash some away in the freezer for another night. Use half for a spaghetti dinner and turn the other half into Baked Ziti with Kale and Olives. No matter how you serve it, this sauce will satisfy the hungriest crowd!

½ pound bacon, diced

1 onion, diced

2 pounds ground beef

2 carrots, diced

1 celery stalk, diced

6 garlic cloves, crushed

2 (24-ounce) cans crushed tomatoes

2 teaspoons dried oregano

2 teaspoons dried basil

2 teaspoons dried thyme

1 teaspoon salt

½ teaspoon black pepper

¼ teaspoon sugar

In a large pot, cook the bacon over medium heat until crisp. Transfer the bacon to a paper towel–lined plate and drain the rendered fat from the pot. Add the onion, ground beef, carrots, celery, and garlic to the pot. Cook, stirring, over medium heat until the beef is cooked through. Add the cooked bacon, crushed tomatoes, oregano, basil, thyme, salt, pepper, and sugar. Stir to combine. Cook over medium heat until heated through.

Tonight: Bolognese Spaghetti

Serves 6 to 8

16 ounces spaghetti

½ recipe Bolognese Sauce

½ cup grated Parmesan cheese

Bring a large pot of water to a boil. Add the spaghetti and cook for 7 to 8 minutes, until al dente.

Meanwhile, in a saucepan, warm the Bolognese Sauce over medium heat until hot.

Drain the pasta and serve topped with the sauce and sprinkled with Parmesan.

Tomorrow: Baked Ziti with Kale and Olives

Serves 6 to 8

Cooking spray

16 ounces ziti

½ recipe Bolognese Sauce

2¼ ounces black olives, pitted and sliced

2 cups baby kale

8 ounces shredded mozzarella cheese

Preheat the oven to 350°F. Spray a 4-quart baking dish with cooking spray.

Bring a large pot of water to a boil. Add the ziti and cook for 11 minutes, until al dente. Drain the pasta. Place the cooked pasta in the prepared baking dish. Spoon half the sauce over the pasta and stir to combine. Layer the olives and kale over the pasta. Spoon the remaining sauce evenly over all. Top with the mozzarella. Bake, uncovered, for 30 minutes, until hot and bubbling.

I WANT TO COOK FOR THE WHOLE WEEK TONIGHT

—

Stocking your freezer with meals has never been easier. If you can carve out an hour to prep these recipes, you can get six meals in the freezer simply and easily. All meals are designed to cook in the slow cooker, and some also have pressure-cooking instructions. Prep on a weekend and use the meals for a week's worth of dinners, or space them out and use them on extra-busy days when you have no time to cook. They're also handy for sharing with a friend. A few months ago, I put six meals in my freezer, and I was later able to share a couple of them with a friend whose baby was born on the same day that her family moved into a new house!

To simplify your prep day, chop all the veggies first. Group each recipe's vegetables together. Place the meat in gallon-size zip-top plastic freezer bags and then add the other ingredients. The exception to this would be for King's Chicken Noodle Soup and Creamy Italian-Style Chicken and Kale Soup—I like using a large bowl for soups so I don't risk a spill in the freezer. If you have a small family of two to four people, you can split the ingredients for any of the recipes between two freezer bags and get two meals instead of one.

I've given you two different plans here. Each one has six recipes and can be finished in about one hour. Sixty minutes to prep six meals is a great use of your time.

For a printable version of the grocery lists, go to eatathome tonight.com/plans. The grocery lists are color-coded to make it easy to see which ingredients go with each meal.

6-in-1 Menu Plan 1 Shopping List

INGREDIENT	CHIPOTLE STEAK TACOS	LAZY MARINATED CHICKEN	KING'S CHICKEN NOODLE SOUP	ITALIAN SAUSAGE AND PEPPERS	MOZZARELLA-STUFFED MEATBALLS	GINGERED PEAR PORK LOIN	TOTAL (GROCERY STORE QUANTITIES)
PRODUCE							
Green bell pepper	1			1			2
Onion	1		1	1	¼ cup minced		4
Garlic	1 clove	1 clove	2 cloves	3 or 4 cloves	4 cloves		11 or 12 cloves, or 1 head
Lettuce	2 cups shredded						1 head, or 2 cups preshredded
Red bell pepper				1			1
Celery			2 stalks				1 head
Carrots			3 or 4				3 or 4
Ginger						2 teaspoons grated fresh (from about one 1-inch knob), or ½ teaspoon ground	1 (1-inch) knob fresh, or 1 small jar ground
Pears						2 or 3	2 or 3
CANNED/DRY							
Fire-roasted diced tomatoes	1 (15-ounce) can						1 (15-ounce) can)
Chipotle peppers in adobo sauce	1 (7-ounce) can						1 (7-ounce) can)
Olive oil		⅓ cup					1 small bottle
Balsamic vinegar		⅓ cup					1 small bottle
Worcestershire sauce		2 tablespoons					1 small bottle
Light brown sugar		¼ cup					1 (16-ounce) package
Dijon mustard		2 teaspoons					1 jar
Crushed tomatoes				1 (28-ounce) can	1 (28-ounce) can + 1 (15-ounce) can		2 (28-ounce) cans + 1 (15-ounce) can
Tomato sauce				1 (8-ounce) can			1 (8-ounce) can
Chicken broth			2 (32-ounce) containers				2 (32-ounce) containers
Egg noodles			3 cups uncooked				1 (16-ounce) bag
Bread crumbs					1 cup		1 small container
Apple juice						½ cup	1 small bottle

INGREDIENT	CHIPOTLE STEAK TACOS	LAZY MARINATED CHICKEN	KING'S CHICKEN NOODLE SOUP	ITALIAN SAUSAGE AND PEPPERS	MOZZARELLA-STUFFED MEATBALLS	GINGERED PEAR PORK LOIN	TOTAL (GROCERY STORE QUANTITIES)
DAIRY							
Cheddar cheese	1 cup shredded						1 cup shredded
Egg					1		1
Mozzarella cheese					4 ounces		4 ounces
MEAT							
Round steak	2 pounds round steak						1 (2-pound)
Boneless chicken breasts or thighs		2½ pounds					2½ pounds
Sweet Italian sausage links				2 pounds			1½ pounds
Bone-in chicken breasts			2 large				2 large
Lean ground beef					2 pounds		2 pounds
Pork tenderloin or pork roast						1 (2- to 3-pound)	1 (2- to 3-pound)
BREAD							
Flour tortillas (6-inch)	10 (6-inch) flour tortillas						10 (6-inch)
PANTRY ITEMS							
Salt	as needed	as needed	as needed	as needed	as needed	as needed	as needed
Black pepper	as needed	as needed	as needed	as needed	as needed	as needed	as needed
Dried oregano			1 tablespoon	2 teaspoons			1 tablespoon + 2 teaspoons
Dried basil			1 tablespoon	1 teaspoon			1 tablespoon + 1 teaspoon
Dried thyme		1 teaspoon	2 teaspoons				3 teaspoons
Bay leaf		1					1

NOTE: For a printable version of the grocery list, go to eatathometonight.com/plans.

Chipotle Steak Tacos

Serves 6 to 8

Tacos are one of my favorite ways to feed a group of hungry people or to feed the group of stragglers who always seems to drift into my kitchen after five o'clock. They're easy, reheat well, and can be customized with various toppings, and everyone (seriously, *everyone*) loves them! These Chipotle Steak Tacos are several notches more interesting than a common taco, but they remain simple to prepare. The chipotle chiles pack some heat, so feel free to add more or less according to your family's tastes. You can also scrape the seeds out of the chiles to lessen their heat considerably while leaving the smoky flavor. This is that recipe you'll want to always have stocked in your freezer for whatever dinner emergencies might strike this week!

2 pounds round steak

1 green bell pepper, sliced

1 onion, sliced

1 garlic clove, crushed

1 (15-ounce) can fire-roasted diced tomatoes, drained

1 (7-ounce) can chipotle chiles in adobo sauce

TO SERVE

10 (6-inch) flour tortillas

1 cup shredded cheddar cheese

2 cups finely shredded lettuce

Place the steak, bell pepper, onion, garlic, and tomatoes in a gallon-size zip-top plastic freezer bag. Remove 1 or 2 chipotle chiles from the can. Halve the chile(s), scrape out the seeds, and finely chop. Add the chipotle to the freezer bag. Measure 1 to 2 teaspoons of the adobo sauce from the can and add to the freezer bag. (Any remaining chipotles and sauce can be frozen for another use.) Close the bag and freeze.

The night before you plan to serve the tacos, set the freezer bag in the refrigerator to thaw. Pour the contents of the bag into a slow cooker. Cover and cook on High for 5 to 6 hours or on Low for 7 to 8 hours. Shred the meat with two forks and serve in tortillas, topped with the cheese and lettuce.

Lazy Marinated Chicken

Serves 6 to 8

Here's what I've figured out—you can marinate chicken while it's still frozen. Someone may tell you that this isn't the proper way to do it, but it works! And what we're after is a quick way to do something that works. Let others spend a lot of time doing things the proper way. You and I are going to make it fast and get on with the part that matters, which is spending time with our families. This chicken can be cooked in a slow cooker, in a skillet on the stovetop, or outside on the grill on a nice day.

2½ pounds frozen boneless, skinless chicken breasts or thighs

⅓ cup olive oil

⅓ cup balsamic vinegar

2 tablespoons Worcestershire sauce

¼ cup packed light brown sugar

2 teaspoons Dijon mustard

1 garlic clove, crushed

Salt and black pepper

Place the chicken (no need to thaw it) in a gallon-size zip-top plastic freezer bag. Combine the oil, vinegar, Worcestershire, brown sugar, mustard, and garlic in a container with a tight-fitting lid. Season with salt and pepper. Close the container and shake to blend the ingredients together. Pour this mixture over the chicken, seal the bag, and freeze.

The night before you plan to serve the chicken, set the freezer bag in the refrigerator to thaw. Pour the contents of the bag into a slow cooker. Cover and cook on High for 5 to 6 hours or on Low 7 to 8 hours.

King's Chicken Noodle Soup

Serves 6 to 8

This classic chicken noodle soup gets its homemade flavor from a slow cooker trick I learned a few years ago. Instead of cooking the chicken separately, I use bone-in chicken breasts that cook in the soup along with the other ingredients. The chicken breasts give the soup a similar flavor to using a whole chicken and making your own broth. It's a much fuller and richer taste than using boneless breasts. This version is so simple to make. Stock your freezer with this recipe and be ready the next time your family needs a bowl of comfort food.

2 large bone-in chicken breasts

2 celery stalks, diced

1 onion, diced

2 garlic cloves, crushed

3 or 4 carrots, chopped

8 cups chicken broth

1 teaspoon dried thyme

1 bay leaf

Salt and black pepper

3 cups uncooked egg noodles, for serving

Place all the ingredients except the noodles in a large freezer-safe bowl with a lid. Close the lid and freeze.

A day or two before you plan to serve the soup, set the bowl in the refrigerator to thaw (this may take up to 48 hours, so plan ahead). Pour the contents of the bowl into a slow cooker. Cover and cook on High for 5 to 6 hours or on Low for 7 to 8 hours. Remove the chicken from the soup, being careful to get all the bones. Pull the meat from the bones and return the meat to the soup; discard the bones. Five to 10 minutes before serving, stir in the egg noodles and allow them to cook in the hot broth.

Italian Sausage and Peppers

Serves 6 to 8

Talk about versatile! There are so many ways you can serve this dish, all of them simple and easy. Try Italian Sausage and Peppers spooned over hot polenta, spaghetti squash, pasta, or cooked grains. Fill the centers of baked acorn squash with sausage and peppers. Pile it on piping-hot baked potatoes. Turn it into a fork-required French bread pizza. No matter how you serve it, the prep is simple. And since it only takes a few minutes to get it in the freezer, you'll have this dish ready to go at all times, just waiting to be turned into whatever you're craving that night.

2 pounds sweet Italian sausage links, sliced into ½-inch-thick rounds

1 red bell pepper, chopped

1 green bell pepper, chopped

1 onion, chopped

3 or 4 garlic cloves, crushed

1 (28-ounce) can crushed tomatoes

1 (8-ounce) can tomato sauce

1 tablespoon dried oregano

1 tablespoon dried basil

2 teaspoons dried thyme

Salt and black pepper

Place all the ingredients in a gallon-size plastic zip-top freezer bag. Seal the bag and freeze.

The night before you plan to serve the sausage and peppers, set the freezer bag in the refrigerator to thaw. Pour the contents of the bag into a slow cooker. Cover and cook on High for 5 to 6 hours or on Low for 7 to 8 hours.

Mozzarella-Stuffed Meatballs

Serves 6 to 8

These are not your ordinary meatballs. First, they are huge! Second, they are filled with gooey mozzarella cheese. The best part is that they are so easy to make, but look impressive enough for guests. Serve these with spaghetti or go for a heartier pasta like penne or rigatoni. We love to turn any leftovers into meatball subs the next day. Just heat, slice, and serve on toasted buns.

2 pounds lean ground beef

1 large egg

¼ cup minced onion

1 cup bread crumbs

Salt and black pepper

4 ounces mozzarella cheese, cut into 10 cubes

1 (28-ounce) can crushed tomatoes plus 1 (15-ounce) can crushed tomatoes

4 garlic cloves, crushed

1 teaspoon dried basil

2 teaspoons dried oregano

In a large bowl, combine the ground beef, egg, onion, and bread crumbs and season with salt and pepper. Divide the meat into 10 equal portions and pat them into thick patties. Press one cube of cheese into the center of each patty. Fold the meat around the cheese to completely enclose it, then shape the meat into a ball. Place the meatballs in a gallon-size plastic zip-top freezer bag.

In a medium bowl, stir together the tomatoes, garlic, basil, and oregano. Pour the mixture over the meatballs. Seal the bag and freeze.

The night before you plan to serve the meatballs, set the freezer bag in the refrigerator to thaw (or defrost the meatballs in the microwave, if you're pressed for time). Pour the contents of the bag into a slow cooker or pressure cooker.

If using a slow cooker, cover and cook on High for 5 to 6 hours or on Low for 7 to 8 hours.

If using a pressure cooker, seal the lid and set the cook time to 20 minutes. Quick-release the pressure.

Gingered Pear Pork Loin

Serves 6 to 8

This recipe couldn't be simpler. If you can peel a pear, you can make this pork loin. The pears give the meat a slightly sweet taste and the ginger gives it a little zing. Still, the flavor is mild, and it's best paired with side dishes that will complement it and add color. Think dark green leafy vegetables—either in a salad or cooked. Baked sweet potatoes or honey-butter carrots (see page 77) will round out the flavors and colors nicely.

1 (2- to 3-pound) pork tenderloin or pork roast

½ cup apple juice

2 teaspoons grated fresh ginger, or ½ teaspoon ground ginger

2 or 3 pears, peeled, cored, and sliced

Salt and black pepper

Place all the ingredients in a gallon-size plastic zip-top freezer bag. Seal the bag and freeze.

The night before you plan to serve the pork, set the freezer bag in the refrigerator to thaw (or defrost the pork in the microwave if you're pressed for time). Pour the contents of the bag into a slow cooker. Cover and cook on High for 5 to 6 hours or on Low for 7 to 8 hours.

6-in-1 Menu Plan 2 Shopping List

INGREDIENT	THE SIMPLEST SWEET-AND-SOUR PORK CHOPS	SPICE RACK SLOW-COOKED TURKEY BREAST	CREAMY PHILLY-ISH CHEESE-STEAKS	MODERN HUNTER CHICKEN CACCIATORE	CREAMY ITALIAN-STYLE CHICKEN AND KALE SOUP	MONGOLIAN BEEF MEATBALLS	TOTAL (GROCERY STORE QUANTITIES)
PRODUCE							
Green bell pepper	1		1	1			3
Onion	1	1	1	1	1		5
Garlic	1 clove		1 clove	3 cloves	3 cloves	2 cloves	10 cloves, or 1 head
Red bell pepper				1	1		2
Celery		2 stalks					1 head
Potatoes					4 large		4 large
Kale					1 large bunch		1 large bunch
Ginger					1 teaspoon grated fresh (from about one 1-inch knob), or ½ teaspoon ground		1 (1-inch) knob fresh, or 1 small jar ground
CANNED/DRY							
Pineapple chunks (in juice)	1 (20-ounce) can						1 (20-ounce) can)
Vinegar	3 table-spoons						3 table-spoons
Light brown sugar	3 table-spoons					½ cup	1 (16-ounce) package
Soy sauce	3 table-spoons					½ cup	¾ cup
Cornstarch	1 tablespoon					1 tablespoon	2 tablespoons
Beef broth			½ cup				½ cup
Crushed tomatoes				1 (28-ounce) can			1 (28-ounce) can
Chicken broth		1 (15-ounce) can			3 (15-ounce) cans		3 (15-ounce) cans
Bread crumbs						1¾ cups	1¾ cups
Worcestershire sauce						1 tablespoon	1 tablespoon
Molasses						1 tablespoon	1 tablespoon

INGREDIENT	THE SIMPLEST SWEET-AND-SOUR PORK CHOPS	SPICE RACK SLOW-COOKED TURKEY BREAST	CREAMY PHILLY-ISH CHEESE-STEAKS	MODERN HUNTER CHICKEN CACCIATORE	CREAMY ITALIAN-STYLE CHICKEN AND KALE SOUP	MONGOLIAN BEEF MEATBALLS	TOTAL (GROCERY STORE QUANTITIES)
DAIRY							
Cream cheese			1 (8-ounce) package				1 (8-ounce) package
Swiss cheese			6 slices				6 slices
Half-and-half					2 cups		2 cups
Parmesan cheese					1 cup shredded		1 cup shredded
Eggs						2 large	2 large
MEAT							
Boneless pork chops	2 to 3 pounds						2 to 3 pounds
Turkey breast		1 (3- to 4-pound)					1 (3- to 4-pound)
Round steak			2 to 3 pounds				2 to 3 pounds
Boneless chicken breasts or tenders				2½ pounds			2½ pounds
Bone-in chicken breasts					2		2
Lean ground beef						2¼ pounds	2¼ pounds
BREAD							
Sub rolls			6				6
PANTRY ITEMS							
Salt	2 teaspoons	as needed	as needed		1 teaspoon	1 teaspoon	as needed
Black pepper	½ teaspoon	as needed	as needed		¼ teaspoon	½ teaspoon	as needed
Paprika	1 teaspoon						1 teaspoon
Dried thyme	1 teaspoon				1 teaspoon		2 teaspoons
Garlic powder	½ teaspoon					½ teaspoon	1 teaspoon
Dried oregano				1 teaspoon	2 teaspoons		3 teaspoons
Dried basil				½ teaspoon	1 teaspoon		1½ teaspoons
Bay leaves				2			2

NOTE: For a printable version of the grocery list, go to eatathometonight.com/plans.

The Simplest Sweet-and-Sour Pork Chops

Serves 6 to 8

I've been making this simple sweet-and-sour sauce since my oldest daughter was very young. As a little girl, she loved China—the food, the language, the culture. She majored in Chinese language in college and lived in China twice for several months. For her birthday she always requests sweet-and-sour chicken, and that's where the sauce recipe originated. Over the years I've used the sauce to create lots of other recipes. None are authentic Chinese food, but all are delicious. These pork chops are no exception. Serve them with steamed rice and add egg rolls and fortune cookies if you want to add to the fun.

2 to 3 pounds boneless pork chops

1 onion, chopped

1 green bell pepper, chopped

1 garlic clove, crushed

1 (20-ounce) can pineapple chunks, drained, juice reserved

3 tablespoons distilled white vinegar

3 tablespoons light brown sugar

3 tablespoons soy sauce

1 tablespoon cornstarch

Place the pork chops, onion, bell pepper, garlic, and pineapple chunks in a gallon-size plastic zip-top freezer bag.

In a small bowl, stir together the reserved pineapple juice, vinegar, brown sugar, soy sauce, and cornstarch. Pour the mixture into the bag with the pork chops. Seal the bag and freeze.

The night before you plan to serve the pork, set the freezer bag in the refrigerator to thaw (or defrost the pork in the microwave if you're pressed for time). Pour the contents of the bag into a slow cooker. Cover and cook on High for 4 to 5 hours or on Low for 6 to 7 hours.

Spice Rack Slow-Cooked Turkey Breast

Serves 6 to 8

This isn't your mom's Thanksgiving turkey. Or maybe, I should say, this one is seasoned more than the typical T-day bird. But turkey shouldn't just be for the holidays. I serve this any time of the year. As a bonus, the leftovers can be frozen and used in soups, casseroles, or any recipe using chicken in the I Only Have 15 Minutes Tonight chapter.

1 (3- to 4-pound) turkey breast

2 teaspoons salt

1 teaspoon paprika

1 teaspoon dried thyme

½ teaspoon black pepper

½ teaspoon garlic powder

1 onion, sliced

2 celery stalks, cut into 3-inch pieces

FOR THE PRESSURE COOKER OPTION

1 (15-ounce) can chicken broth

Place the turkey breast in a gallon-size plastic zip-top freezer bag and sprinkle with the salt, paprika, thyme, pepper, and garlic powder. Add the onion and celery to the bag. Seal the bag and freeze.

The night before you plan to serve the turkey, set the freezer bag in the refrigerator to thaw (or defrost the turkey in the microwave if you're pressed for time). Pour the contents of the bag into a slow cooker or pressure cooker.

If using a slow cooker, cover and cook on High for 5 to 6 hours or on Low for 7 to 8 hours.

If using a pressure cooker, add the broth. Seal the lid and set the cook time to 45 minutes. Quick-release the pressure.

Creamy Philly-ish Cheesesteaks

Serves 6

When Jim and I were first married, we lived near Philadelphia. We quickly learned what makes a real Philly cheesesteak and how to order one. You won't find Swiss cheese, Provolone, or green peppers on a true cheesesteak. Instead, the steak is smothered with Cheez Whiz, and your option is to order the sandwich "with" or "without"—onions, that is. It's also fine to eat your steak with ketchup. I found all this surprising, but oh my—those cheesesteaks are amazing, and it's impossible to get a true cheesesteak outside of Philadelphia. The recipe here is nothing like the original, but it's still a crowd-pleaser!

2 to 3 pounds round steak

1 green bell pepper, sliced

1 onion, sliced

1 garlic clove, crushed

½ cup beef broth

Salt and black pepper

TO SERVE

1 (8-ounce) package cream cheese

6 sub rolls

6 slices Swiss cheese

Place the steak, bell pepper, onion, garlic, and broth in gallon-size plastic zip-top freezer bag. Season with salt and black pepper. Seal the bag and freeze.

The night before you plan to serve the cheesesteaks, set the freezer bag in the refrigerator to thaw (or defrost the steak in the microwave if you're pressed for time). Pour the contents of the bag into a slow cooker. Cover and cook on High for 4 to 5 hours or on Low for 6 to 7 hours.

Pull the meat apart with two forks. Stir the cream cheese into the meat and broth in the slow cooker and allow the cream cheese to melt.

Serve the meat on the buns, topped with the Swiss cheese.

Modern Hunter Chicken Cacciatore

Serves 6 to 8

The word *cacciatore* means "hunter" in Italian. The dish is named after the tradition that the chicken was cooked "hunter-style," with herbs, onions, and other vegetables that could be found in the field. You and I are more likely to do our hunting in the aisles of the grocery or even on a shop-at-home website. This modern age has its advantages! That doesn't mean we can't use our modern methods on an old dish. Combining new with the old yields a simple recipe that your family will love. Use your imagination and the contents of your pantry for what to serve with it. Pasta, mashed potatoes, polenta, and risotto are all possibilities.

2½ pounds boneless, skinless chicken breasts or tenders

1 onion, sliced

1 red bell pepper, sliced

1 green bell pepper, sliced

1 (28-ounce) can crushed tomatoes

3 garlic cloves, crushed

1 teaspoon dried oregano

½ teaspoon dried basil

2 bay leaves

Salt and black pepper

Place all the ingredients in a gallon-size plastic zip-top freezer bag. Seal the bag and freeze.

The night before you plan to serve the chicken, set the freezer bag in the refrigerator to thaw (or defrost the chicken in the microwave if you're pressed for time). Pour the contents of the bag into a slow cooker or pressure cooker.

If using a slow cooker, cover and cook on High for 5 to 6 hours or on Low for 7 to 8 hours.

If using a pressure cooker, seal the lid and set the cook time to 12 to 15 minutes. Quick-release the pressure.

Creamy Italian-Style Chicken and Kale Soup

Serves 6 to 8

This creamy chicken soup gets an Italian spin with the seasonings and Parmesan topping. Hearty bowls filled with potatoes, chicken, and kale will warm you on the coldest of days. There are a couple of ingredients that get added at the end of cooking, but this still works for a freezer recipe. Just make a note when you freeze the soup so you remember those extra ingredients.

2 bone-in chicken breasts

4 large potatoes, peeled and chopped

1 onion, diced

1 red bell pepper, chopped

3 garlic cloves, crushed

2 teaspoons dried oregano

1 teaspoon dried basil

1 teaspoon dried thyme

1 teaspoon kosher salt

¼ teaspoon black pepper

3 (15-ounce) cans chicken broth

TO SERVE

1 large bunch kale leaves, chopped

2 cups half-and-half, warmed

1 cup shredded Parmesan cheese

Place the chicken breasts in a large freezer-safe bowl with a lid. Add the potatoes, onion, bell pepper, garlic, oregano, basil, thyme, salt, black pepper, and broth. Cover the bowl and freeze.

A day or two before you plan to serve the soup, set the bowl in the refrigerator to thaw (this may take up to 48 hours, so plan ahead or defrost the soup in the microwave if you're pressed for time). Pour the contents of the bowl into a slow cooker. Cover and cook on High for 5 to 6 hours or on Low for 7 to 8 hours.

Carefully remove the chicken from the slow cooker and pull the meat from the bones. Return the meat to the slow cooker and discard the bones. Add the kale and half-and-half. Cook for 10 minutes more, until the soup is heated through and the kale has wilted a bit.

Serve in bowls, topped with the Parmesan.

Mongolian Beef Meatballs

Serves 6 to 8

Don't be put off by the longer ingredient list for this recipe. It comes together very fast and easily, which is a good thing, because your family is going to ask for this one often. The dish has the flavors of your favorite takeout meal, but the convenience of a freezer recipe. Serve the meatballs over rice, with plenty of steamed broccoli on the side.

2¼ pounds lean ground beef

1¾ cups bread crumbs

2 large eggs

1 teaspoon salt

½ teaspoon garlic powder

½ teaspoon black pepper

1 tablespoon Worcestershire sauce

1 teaspoon grated fresh ginger, or
   ¼ teaspoon ground ginger

2 garlic cloves, crushed

½ cup soy sauce

½ cup packed light brown sugar

1 tablespoon molasses

TO SERVE

1 tablespoon cornstarch

In a large bowl, combine the ground beef, bread crumbs, eggs, salt, garlic powder, pepper, and Worcestershire. Mix with your hands until thoroughly blended. Roll the mixture into meatballs about 1½ inches in diameter. Place the meatballs in a gallon-size zip-top plastic freezer bag.

In a medium bowl, stir together the ginger, garlic, soy sauce, brown sugar, molasses, and ½ cup water. Pour the mixture over the meatballs. Seal the bag and freeze.

The night before you plan to serve the meatballs, set the freezer bag in the refrigerator to thaw (or defrost the meatballs in the microwave if you're pressed for time). Pour the contents of the bag into a slow cooker. Cover and cook on High for 5 to 6 hours or on Low for 7 to 8 hours.

Ten minutes before serving, ladle ⅓ cup of the sauce into a measuring cup. Stir the cornstarch into the sauce until well blended, then pour the sauce back into the slow cooker and stir to thicken all the sauce.

HOW TO COOK CHICKEN
FOR THE FREEZER

My favorite quick-cooking tip is to keep cooked chicken in the freezer. This one step can mean the difference between a meal that takes forty-five minutes or more and one that you can have on the table in just fifteen minutes.

Freeze shredded or chopped cooked chicken in plastic freezer bags in 1- to 3-cup quantities. If you're really pressed for time, you can pull rotisserie chicken meat from the bones and chop or shred it with two forks, then freeze it, but it's very easy to cook and freeze your own. Consider cooking a whole chicken and eating some for dinner, then freezing the rest. Chicken stored in the freezer will last 4 to 6 months.

You can use the oven to cook the chicken, but I prefer to use the slow cooker or, more recently, the pressure cooker. Here are simple instructions for each.

Slow Cooker Chicken for the Freezer

Use boneless or bone-in chicken breasts or a whole chicken. Season chicken with salt and pepper. Add water if you'd like to have chicken broth to freeze. Cover and cook on High for 5 to 6 hours or Low for 7 to 8 hours.

Pressure Cooker Chicken for the Freezer

Use boneless or bone-in chicken breasts or a whole chicken. Season with salt and pepper. Add at least 2 cups water. Seal the lid and set the cook time to 10 to 12 minutes for boneless, 15 minutes for bone-in, or 25 to 30 minutes for a whole chicken. Do a quick pressure release before opening the lid.

I HAVE A BIT MORE TIME TONIGHT

———

When I first learned to cook, I loved spending an hour or more cooking a meal. It was a fun hobby that had immediate gratification in the form of a delicious dinner. Once I had a family to cook for and the task became a three-times-a-day event, the focus became quick meals instead of relaxed cooking sessions.

The recipes in this chapter strike a balance between super-fast meals and overly involved recipes. They won't take you a long time to cook, but they require a bit more time than the other recipes in this book. Save them for the weekend or a night when your schedule feels freer.

There's something about settling in for a good cooking session that makes me feel like I have all the time in the world. When I let myself focus solely on the food and the people who may be wandering in and out of the kitchen, I experience a peace that is often missing in the rush of daily life.

I'm sure that has to do with giving myself time to do something I enjoy. Setting aside technology for a while doesn't hurt, either. And there's something about the sensory experience of cooking—the scents, tastes, sounds, and physical activity of chopping, stirring, searing, and more—that is a balm to nerves frayed by busyness and too much social media scrolling.

Pull out the cutting board and a sharp knife. Choose one of the recipes in this chapter and give yourself a chance to enjoy cooking for the people you love.

One-Pot Baked Chicken and Tortellini

Serves 6 to 8

This is one of my favorite ways to fix a whole chicken. There's something comforting about a chicken dinner, and adding pasta to that ups the comfort level even more. In this simple recipe, the tortellini are added to the Dutch oven after the chicken has finished cooking, infusing the pasta with the delicious and hearty flavors of the broth. This not only means one less pan to clean, but it doubles the flavor you'll get from the tortellini. That's what I call a simple and elegant dinner!

3 tablespoons olive oil

4 garlic cloves, crushed

1 whole (5- to 6-pound) chicken

2 (15-ounce) cans diced tomatoes

1 (14-ounce) can artichoke hearts, drained and rinsed

1 tablespoon Italian seasoning

Salt and black pepper

2 (9-ounce) packages refrigerated tortellini

Parmesan cheese, grated, for serving

Preheat the oven to 350°F.

In a large Dutch oven, heat the oil over medium heat until hot but not smoking. Add the garlic and cook for 1 to 2 minutes. Add the whole chicken to the pot, breast-side down. Cook for about 5 minutes to brown the first side, then turn the chicken over and cook for about 5 minutes to brown the second side. Add the tomatoes with their juices, artichoke hearts, Italian seasoning, and 1 cup water and season with salt and pepper.

Cover and bake for 1¼ to 1½ hours. Remove from the oven and add the tortellini to the pot, using a spoon to submerge the pasta under the broth. Cover and let stand for 3 to 5 minutes. Remove the chicken from the pot and carve the meat from the bones.

Serve the chicken with the tortellini, artichokes, and tomatoes, and top with Parmesan.

My Favorite
Chicken and Dumplings

Serves 6

This recipe delivers comfort from the moment you set the mixing bowl, rolling pin, and ingredients on the counter until you lift the chicken and steaming dumplings to your mouth. The recipe for these Southern-style dumplings came to me from my mom, but it started with my aunt Lois. The dough is rolled and cut, then boiled in broth. The result is thicker than a noodle, but not as thick as a drop dumpling, and you won't find any vegetables in these. In my house, Thanksgiving requires a heaping bowl as part of the feast—made with turkey, of course—but we have them at other times of the year, too.

2½ to 3 pounds bone-in chicken breasts

1½ teaspoons salt

2 cups all-purpose flour, plus more for dusting

½ teaspoon baking powder

2 tablespoons salted butter

¾ cup plus 2 tablespoons milk

1 (32-ounce) container chicken broth

Pressure Cooker

Put the chicken, 1 teaspoon of the salt, and 4 cups water in a pressure cooker. Seal the lid and set the cook time to 25 minutes. Quick-release the pressure.

Slow Cooker

Put the chicken, 1 teaspoon of the salt, and 4 cups water in a slow cooker. Cover and cook on High for 5 to 6 hours or on Low for 7 to 8 hours.

Stovetop

Put the chicken in a large pot and add 1 teaspoon of the salt and water to cover. Bring the water to a boil, then lower the heat and simmer for 1 hour, or until the chicken is cooked through.

(recipe continues)

While the chicken cooks, in a large bowl, stir together the flour, baking powder, and remaining ½ teaspoon salt. Cut the butter into the dry ingredients using a fork or pastry blender until it forms soft crumbs. Add the milk and stir with a fork until a soft dough forms.

Generously flour the counter. Place the dough on the counter and pat it into a small, thick rectangle, folding it in half and turning it to lightly knead it several times. Flour a rolling pin and roll out the dough to about ¼ inch thick. Use a pizza cutter or butter knife to cut roughly 2-inch square dumplings. Don't worry about making them all exactly the same size. Place the dumplings on a plate, flouring and separating each layer with waxed paper.

Once the chicken is cooked (by any of the three cooking methods), remove it from the cooking liquid and pull the meat from the bones. Set the meat aside and discard the bones.

In a large saucepan, combine the broth and 2 cups of the chicken cooking liquid and bring to a boil. Drop the dumplings into the boiling broth one at a time, stirring as you add each. Raise the heat to medium-high and boil for 15 to 20 minutes. The dumplings are done when they no longer look doughy in the center. Remove from the heat and stir the chicken meat into the broth. Serve in bowls.

Chicago Pizza Potpie

Serves 6 to 8

Several years ago, I went to Chicago to visit a friend who lived there. She led us through snowy, windy streets to a cozy pizza place crowded with waiting people. The specialty there is pizza potpie, and I've been trying to re-create it ever since. Despite my efforts, I haven't been able to duplicate the original, but this recipe is a crowd-pleaser anyway! My kids often request it for birthday dinners. Instead of making individual servings, which is more time-consuming and requires ovenproof bowls, I opt for a large casserole dish. This could be called upside-down pizza, because it gets assembled in the reverse order of a normal pizza— cheese on the bottom, topped by lots of meaty sauce, blanketed with pizza dough.

FOR THE FILLING

Olive oil, for greasing the dish

1 pound bulk mild Italian sausage

1 pound lean ground beef

1 onion, diced

3 garlic cloves, crushed

1 (15-ounce) can crushed tomatoes

1 tablespoon dried oregano

2 teaspoons dried basil

½ teaspoon garlic powder

1 teaspoon salt

Black pepper

2 to 3 cups shredded mozzarella

FOR THE PIZZA DOUGH

2¼ teaspoons rapid-rise yeast

1 cup warm water

1 teaspoon sugar

½ teaspoon kosher salt

2 tablespoons olive oil

2½ cups bread flour (see Notes, page 143), plus more for dusting

1 tablespoon salted butter, melted

½ teaspoon dried oregano

½ teaspoon dried basil

(recipe continues)

Preheat the oven to 425°F.

Grease a 9 × 13-inch casserole dish well with oil.

In a large skillet, combine the sausage, ground beef, onion, and garlic and cook over medium heat until the sausage and beef are browned. Drain off any excess grease. Add the tomatoes, oregano, basil, garlic powder, and salt and season with pepper. Cook over medium heat until hot and bubbling. Sprinkle the mozzarella evenly over the bottom of the prepared casserole dish. Ladle the filling over the cheese.

For the pizza dough (see Notes), in the bowl of a stand mixer fitted with the dough hook, dissolve the yeast in the warm water. Add the sugar, kosher salt, olive oil, and bread flour. Mix on medium-low speed until well combined. Let the dough rest 5 minutes.

On a well-floured surface, roll out the dough into a 9 × 13-inch rectangle. Gently lift the dough and place it over the casserole dish, pressing it to the rim of the dish to seal. Trim any extra dough from around the edges of the dish. Brush the melted butter over the dough and sprinkle with the oregano and basil. Bake for 25 minutes, until the dough is golden brown.

To serve, invert portions onto plates, turning them upside down so the cheese ends up on top.

NOTES You can use all-purpose flour instead of bread flour, but the dough will turn out a bit better with bread flour.

Also, this dough can be made by hand if you don't have a mixer. Combine the ingredients in a large bowl and then knead the dough by hand for 2 to 3 minutes.

New Year's Day Beef Vegetable Soup

Serves 10 to 12

When I was little, my mom would make this beef vegetable soup on a lazy, cold day. I remember having it on New Year's Day many times. We would spend the day in our pajamas, playing marathon games of Monopoly and eating bowl after bowl of this soup. This recipe does take some time to make since the beef needs to be cooked separately from the rest of the soup. The result is worth the effort, though. To make it simple, I've given instructions below for cooking the beef roast in either a slow cooker or a pressure cooker. I've also included instructions for using both appliances for finishing the soup, but it can also be finished on the stovetop. If you have extra servings, just transfer the soup to freezer-safe containers and freeze the leftovers for another meal.

1 (2½- to 3-pound) bone-in beef roast

Salt and black pepper

5 medium potatoes, peeled and cubed

5 carrots, halved lengthwise and sliced

1 large onion, diced

1 (15-ounce) can diced tomatoes

1 (15-ounce) can tomato sauce

1 (32-ounce) container beef broth

1 (12-ounce) bag frozen corn kernels

1 cup fresh or frozen cut green beans

Place the beef in a pressure cooker or slow cooker. Season with salt and pepper and add water to cover.

If using a pressure cooker, seal the lid and set the cook time to 50 minutes. Quick-release the pressure.

If using a slow cooker, cover and cook on High for 5 to 6 hours or on Low for 7 to 8 hours.

When finished, remove the roast from the cooking liquid and shred the meat with two forks. At this point, you can refrigerate or freeze the meat and the cooking liquid separately to finish later, or finish the soup now.

To finish the soup, return the meat to the cooking liquid in the pressure cooker or slow cooker. (If you've frozen the meat and cooking liquid, thaw them in the refrigerator, then combine them in a large saucepan.) Add the potatoes, carrots, onion, diced tomatoes with their juices, tomato sauce, broth, corn, green beans, 2 teaspoons salt, ½ teaspoon pepper, and 2 cups water.

If using a pressure cooker, seal the lid and set the cook time to 30 minutes. Quick-release the pressure before removing the lid.

If using a slow cooker, cover and cook on High for 5 to 6 hours or on Low for 7 to 8 hours.

If you're finishing the soup on the stovetop, bring the soup to a boil and then reduce the heat to simmer for 30 minutes, until the potatoes are tender. Reduce the heat to low and simmer until ready to serve.

Taste and adjust the seasoning before serving, adding more salt and pepper if needed.

Mexican Meat Loaf

Serves 6 to 8

On a recent visit to Austin, Texas, we ate at a restaurant that had Mexican meat loaf on the menu. That intrigued me, but I didn't order it (hello, chicken enchiladas!). I knew I'd be able to create a version of the Tex-Mex meat loaf at home, and I loved the challenge of doing so. It's a free-form loaf, studded with diced bell peppers, seasoned with chiles and cumin, stuffed with cheese, and topped with savory sauce and more cheese. Serve this with Loaded Smashed Potatoes (page 191).

2¼ pounds lean ground beef

1 large egg

1 (10-ounce) can diced tomatoes with green chiles, drained

¼ cup diced onion

¼ cup diced red bell pepper

¼ cup diced green bell pepper

¾ cup bread crumbs

½ teaspoon chili powder

¼ teaspoon ground cumin

½ teaspoon salt, plus more as needed

¼ teaspoon black pepper, plus more as needed

1½ cups grated Monterey Jack cheese

1 (8-ounce) can tomato sauce

½ teaspoon garlic powder

Preheat the oven to 375°F. Line a 9 × 13-inch baking pan with aluminum foil.

In a large bowl, combine the ground beef, egg, tomatoes with green chiles, onion, bell peppers, bread crumbs, chili powder, cumin, salt, and black pepper. Use your hands to mix (you can also do this in the bowl of a stand mixer using the paddle attachment, if you have one). Divide the meat mixture into two equal parts. Lightly press half the meat in the center of the pan to make a loaf shape in the center. Place ¾ cup of the cheese evenly over the center of the meat mixture. Be careful to keep the cheese inside the edges of the meat. Use the remaining meat to form the top of the loaf, sandwiching the cheese in the middle to enclose it fully inside the meat. Pat firmly to form a loaf. Cover with foil and bake for 1½ hours.

Meanwhile, in a small bowl, stir together the tomato sauce and garlic powder and season with salt and pepper.

Remove the meat loaf from the oven, uncover it, and pour the sauce over the top. Sprinkle the remaining ¾ cup cheese over the sauce. Return the meat loaf to the oven and bake for 15 minutes more.

Remove from the oven and place the meat loaf on a serving plate.

Italian Skillet Chicken with Tomatoes and Spinach over Parmesan Pasta

Serves 4 to 6

The instructions for this recipe look a bit longer, but I promise it is easy. You can have the whole meal ready in about thirty minutes. Pair it with garlic bread and a green salad, and you have a meal fit for company that's still simple enough for an ordinary Tuesday night.

1½ to 2 pounds boneless, skinless chicken breasts

Salt and black pepper

2 to 3 tablespoons olive oil

1 onion, chopped

3 garlic cloves, crushed

1 (15-ounce) can diced tomatoes, lightly drained

1 teaspoon dried oregano

1 teaspoon dried basil

1 teaspoon dried thyme

1 pound angel hair pasta

½ cup shredded Parmesan cheese

2 cups fresh spinach

Season the chicken with salt and pepper. In a large skillet, heat the oil over medium heat. Add the chicken and brown on both sides, about 5 minutes per side. Transfer the chicken to a plate. Add the onion and garlic to the skillet and cook for 2 to 3 minutes. Pour the tomatoes into the skillet and add the oregano, basil, and thyme. Return the chicken to the skillet. Cover and cook until the chicken is cooked through, 15 to 20 minutes.

Meanwhile, bring a large pot of water to a boil. Salt the water, add the pasta, and cook for 5 to 6 minutes, until al dente. Near the end of the cooking time, dip out 1 to 2 cups of the pasta cooking water and set it aside. Drain the pasta and return it to the pot. Add the cheese and toss, pouring in a bit of the reserved cooking water to keep the pasta from being dry.

Add the spinach to the skillet with the chicken, cover, and cook for 3 to 5 minutes, until the spinach is wilted.

Serve the chicken on a bed of the Parmesan pasta.

Kentucky's Finest Hot Chicken and Corn Waffles

Serves 6

Chicken and waffles may sound like an odd combination, but it is delicious! The chicken breading includes hot sauce, which brings a little heat to the dish (don't worry—you can easily adjust the heat to suit your family's tastes). The savory corn waffles don't have the sweet flavor of breakfast waffles, but are delicious with the chicken. And maple syrup brings a bit of sweetness to contrast with the spiciness of the chicken. Instead of frying in oil, I chose an oven-fry method.

FOR THE CHICKEN

½ cup (1 stick) salted butter, melted

1 to 4 teaspoons hot sauce, depending on how hot you like it

1 cup all-purpose flour

½ cup panko bread crumbs

1 teaspoon salt

¼ teaspoon black pepper

¼ teaspoon garlic powder

⅛ teaspoon onion powder

⅛ teaspoon paprika

1½ pounds chicken tenders

Vegetable oil, for frying (optional)

FOR THE CORN WAFFLES

1½ cups all-purpose flour

2 teaspoons baking powder

½ teaspoon salt

1½ cups milk

4 tablespoons (½ stick) salted butter, melted and cooled

3 large eggs, separated

½ cup frozen corn kernels, thawed

Maple syrup, for serving

For the chicken, preheat the oven to 425°F. Line a baking sheet with aluminum foil.

Stir the melted butter and hot sauce together in a shallow dish. (With 1 teaspoon hot sauce, there's little to no heat. If you like it spicier, add more.)

In a separate shallow dish, combine flour, panko, salt, pepper, garlic powder, onion powder, and paprika. Dip the chicken first in the butter mixture, then in the seasoned flour. Place the coated chicken on the prepared baking sheet. Bake for 20 to 30 minutes, until the chicken is cooked through.

(recipe continues)

If you prefer crispier chicken, in a heavy-bottomed skillet, heat about 1 inch of oil over medium-high heat. Test the oil: if a pinch of panko sizzles on contact, it's ready. Add the chicken and fry 4 to 5 minutes on each side, until the chicken is browned and the inside is cooked through.

For the waffles, preheat a waffle iron according to the manufacturer's instructions.

In a large bowl, stir together the flour, baking powder, and salt. In a separate small bowl, stir together the milk, melted butter, and egg yolks.

In the bowl of a stand mixer fitted with the whisk attachment, beat the egg whites on high speed until they hold peaks.

Add the milk mixture to the flour mixture and stir gently until well combined. Gently fold in the beaten egg whites, then fold in the corn.

Ladle ½ cup of the batter onto the hot waffle iron and cook according to the manufacturer's instructions. Transfer the waffle to a plate and repeat with the remaining batter.

To serve, place chicken on top of a waffle. Drizzle with maple syrup.

Tomato Goat Cheese Quiche

Serves 6

I know I've mentioned our trip to Paris already in this book, but I'm going to do it again. (Remember, one of my life mottoes is "Take the trip," meaning take those opportunities that come up, even if the timing doesn't seem ideal. The memories will be worth it.) One day at lunch we visited a bakery someone had recommended to us. The day was gray and drizzly and there was a line to order food. In France, if you want to sit inside at the tables, you go in and sit. If you stand in the line and order, you can't sit inside. For some reason, this threw us off track several times. We're more used to ordering at a counter and then finding a seat. On this gray, misty day we made this mistake again and ended up sitting on a street bench with our lunch. Considering the excellent setting and the warm baguette, it wasn't much of a mistake! One of the things we ordered was a quiche that had tomatoes and some type of cheese. We didn't know how to ask for it warm, so we ate it cold and we loved it! That's the quiche I had in mind when I created this one. It's not an exact re-creation, of course, and the setting will be different, but make it and ponder what "trip" you need to take.

1 cup all-purpose flour, plus more for dusting

½ teaspoon salt, plus more as needed

½ cup (1 stick) salted butter

1 cup crumbled goat cheese

1 large tomato, sliced

¼ cup shaved or shredded Parmesan cheese

4 large eggs, beaten

2 cups half-and-half

Black pepper

Preheat the oven to 400°F.

In a large bowl, stir together the flour and salt. Using a fork or pastry blender, cut in the butter to form crumbs. Stir in 2 tablespoons plus 2 teaspoons water with the fork. Keep stirring until the dough comes together to form a ball.

Flour the counter very well and place the dough on the counter. Use a floured rolling pin to roll the dough out to a circle ¼ inch thick. Place the dough in a 9-inch

(recipe continues)

pie plate and crimp the edges. Prick the bottom all over with a fork and bake for 3 minutes. Remove from the oven, prick again, and bake for 5 minutes more.

Remove the piecrust from the oven; keep the oven on. Spread the crumbled goat cheese over the bottom of the crust. Arrange the sliced tomatoes evenly over the goat cheese and sprinkle the Parmesan over the tomatoes.

In a medium bowl, stir together the beaten eggs and half-and-half. Season with salt and pepper. Pour the eggs over the tomatoes in the piecrust. Gently return the pie plate to the oven. Reduce the oven temperature to 350°F and bake for 45 minutes.

Remove from the oven and let rest for 5 to 10 minutes before cutting and serving.

Steak Smothered in Balsamic-Garlic Tomatoes with Feta

Serves 4 to 6

Well-seasoned steak in the skillet, topped with tomatoes, a dash of balsamic vinegar, and crumbled feta cheese, makes a restaurant-worthy meal. This one is easy to make and can be done in about forty-five minutes, including the time to let the steaks come to room temperature. I like to serve this with angel hair pasta on the side, but baked potatoes would also be a good option.

2 pounds steak, your choice of cut

4 garlic cloves: 1 halved, 3 crushed

Kosher salt and black pepper

2 to 3 tablespoons olive oil

4 medium tomatoes, chopped

2 tablespoons balsamic vinegar

1 cup crumbled feta cheese

Allow the steak to come to room temperature for 20 minutes before cooking. Rub the cut sides of the halved garlic clove over both sides of the steak. Discard the garlic clove. Season the steak with salt and pepper.

In a large skillet, heat 2 tablespoons oil over medium-high heat. Add the steak and cook for 2 minutes. Flip and cook for 2 minutes on the second side. Reduce the heat to medium and cook for 2 to 4 minutes more for medium-rare. Add another minute or two if you prefer well done. Remove the steak from the skillet.

Heat another tablespoon of oil in the skillet, if needed. Add the crushed garlic and the tomatoes. Cook, stirring often, for about 5 minutes. Add the vinegar and season with salt and pepper.

Serve the steak topped with the tomatoes and crumbled feta.

Autumn Chicken Skillet with Cranberries, Pecans, and Gorgonzola

Serves 4 to 6

For me, the flavor combination in this recipe is near perfection. The sweet taste of dried cranberries and tang of the Gorgonzola are mouth-watering, especially with the nutty crunch of the pecans! If you're looking for a special meal that is easy to make, this is your recipe. Pair it with a big, green salad topped with raspberry balsamic dressing.

2 pounds boneless, skinless chicken breasts

Salt and black pepper

3 tablespoons olive oil

1 cup 100% apple juice

⅓ cup dried cranberries

⅓ cup chopped pecans

½ cup crumbled Gorgonzola cheese

Season the chicken with salt and pepper on both sides.

In a large skillet, heat the oil over medium heat. Add the chicken and cook for 5 minutes on each side, until browned. Add the apple juice, cover, and cook for 12 to 15 minutes, until the chicken is cooked through. Uncover and sprinkle the chicken with the cranberries, pecans, and Gorgonzola. Cover and cook for 2 minutes, letting the cheese melt.

WE CAN'T SIT DOWN FOR A MEAL TONIGHT

——

One of the biggest challenges that families have in trying to establish the habit of eating at home is that there are so many nights when they aren't home! I understand that. It's so easy to fall into the habit of picking up food when you find yourself away from your kitchen that even when you do have a night at home the default becomes a restaurant meal.

But with a little planning, you can bring your dinner along with you. It won't take long for the benefits to make themselves known. Your "picnic" meal will taste better, be better for you, and cost a lot less, too. You'll also be building the habit of eating at (or from) home.

If you find yourself needing to pack several meals a week, keep a bag of paper plates, napkins, forks, and wet wipes in your car so you don't have to remember them each time.

These recipes work equally well for packed lunches!

Broccoli-Tomato Pasta Salad with Mozzarella Cubes

Serves 6 to 8

I've eaten this salad at soccer games more times than I can count. Showing up on the sidelines with homemade pasta salad will make you quite the center of attention, let me tell you. All the other parents either are still hungrily waiting for their dinner or stopped by a drive-through for burgers on their way to the game. This salad is not only a lot healthier than fast food, but it tastes a whole lot better, too. The simple vinaigrette pairs well with the broccoli, tomatoes, and tortellini, but you could easily substitute other vegetables you have on hand.

16 ounces medium pasta shells

1 large head broccoli, chopped into 1-inch pieces

3 medium tomatoes, chopped

8 ounces mozzarella cheese, cut into ½-inch cubes

½ cup olive oil

¼ cup red wine vinegar

1 garlic clove, crushed

1 tablespoon Dijon mustard

Handful of fresh basil, chopped

¼ teaspoon salt

⅛ teaspoon black pepper

Bring a large pot of salted water to a boil. Add the pasta and cook according to the package directions until al dente. Two to 3 minutes before the end of the pasta cooking time, add the broccoli to the pot. Drain both the pasta and broccoli and rinse with cold water to stop the cooking process. Transfer to a large bowl and add the tomatoes and mozzarella.

In a container with a tight-fitting lid, combine the oil, vinegar, garlic, mustard, basil, salt, and pepper. Seal and shake until well combined, then pour over the salad and toss to coat.

Open-Sesame Magic Chinese Chicken Salad

Serves 6 to 8

Like several of the recipes in the I Only Have 15 Minutes Tonight chapter, this one makes use of cooked chicken (see page 133 for tips on cooking and freezing chicken). You can also use rotisserie chicken in this salad. In fact, this recipe could easily have been filed with the other fifteen-minute meals, but I decided to keep it here because it packs really well. It's magic to find a salad that stays crunchy once the dressing has been added, but that's exactly what you'll find with this one. That quality makes it perfect to make ahead and pack for lunch or a dinner on the sidelines.

1 head napa cabbage, coarsely shredded

2 carrots, diced

3 green onions (scallions), chopped

1 (8-ounce) can sliced water chestnuts, drained

8 ounces fresh snow peas

2 to 3 cups chopped cooked chicken

¼ cup soy sauce

1 tablespoon sesame oil

5 tablespoons distilled white vinegar

¼ cup olive oil

2 tablespoons honey

In a large bowl, toss together the cabbage, carrots, green onions, water chestnuts, snow peas, and chicken.

In a small container with a tight-fitting lid, combine the soy sauce, sesame oil, vinegar, olive oil, and honey. Seal the container and shake well to combine. Pour the dressing over the salad. Toss the salad to coat with the dressing.

Sports-Ready Hummus Wraps with Veggies and Feta

Serves 4

Hummus is a natural take-along food. It holds up well and you can dip all kinds of things into it—carrots, celery, red bell pepper strips, cucumbers, pretzels, pitas, tortilla chips . . . endless possibilities! But hummus also makes a really great wrap filling. You'll feel healthy and smart when you're eating this on the sidelines instead of grabbing fast food at a drive-through.

4 large (10-inch) flour tortillas

¾ cup Easy Basic Hummus (recipe follows)

½ cup chopped cucumber

½ red bell pepper, sliced

1 cup baby spinach

¼ cup diced red onion

½ cup crumbled feta cheese

Spread each tortilla with 3 tablespoons of the hummus. Evenly divide the cucumber, bell pepper, spinach, onion, and feta among the tortillas. Wrap the tortillas around the hummus and veggies. Enjoy!

EASY BASIC HUMMUS

Makes 3¾ cups

2 (15-ounce) cans chickpeas: 1 drained and 1 undrained

¼ cup tahini

2 garlic cloves

2 tablespoons olive oil

¼ cup lemon juice

1 teaspoon ground cumin

Salt and black pepper

Place all the ingredients in a high-speed blender or food processer and process until smooth. Store in an airtight container in the refrigerator for 3 to 5 days, or freeze for up to 6 months.

Turkey, Apple, and Gorgonzola Salad with Honey-Dijon Vinaigrette

Serves 4 to 6

Of all the meals I pack for soccer games and other picnics, I think this is my favorite. There's something about the combination of cool lettuce, crisp apple, creamy Gorgonzola, and the simple dressing that makes me feel like I could eat mountains of this salad! Pack the dressing separately from the salad and drizzle it over the greens just before you're ready to eat, so the greens stay crisp.

1 large head romaine lettuce, torn into bite-size pieces

5 ounces thinly sliced deli turkey, cut into bite-size pieces

1 Granny Smith apple, cored and thinly sliced

¼ cup crumbled Gorgonzola cheese

¼ cup chopped pecans

¼ cup dried cranberries

¼ cup very thinly sliced red onion

¼ cup olive oil

2 tablespoons red wine vinegar

1 tablespoon Dijon mustard

1 tablespoon honey

Salt and black pepper

In a large bowl, combine the lettuce, turkey, apple, Gorgonzola, pecans, cranberries, and onion.

In a small container with a tight-fitting lid, combine the oil, vinegar, mustard, and honey and season with salt and pepper. Seal the container and shake well to combine.

Right before serving, pour the dressing over the salad.

Quinoa Salad with Chicken and Spinach

Serves 6

I cook a lot, and my kids have eaten many, many different things I've made, but this is the recipe that my youngest daughter declared my "best ever." She even ate it for breakfast! While I'm not suggesting you have to eat it as your first meal of the day, I do know you'll be really glad you packed it for your lunch or dinner. This recipe holds up well in the fridge, so you can fix it and then enjoy it for several days.

1 cup uncooked quinoa

1 pound chicken tenders

Salt and black pepper

½ cup plus 2 to 3 tablespoons olive oil

1 red bell pepper, diced

¼ cup white wine vinegar

1 garlic clove, crushed

2 teaspoons Dijon mustard

1 teaspoon dried oregano

1 teaspoon dried basil

3 cups baby spinach

Bring 2 cups water to a boil in a saucepan. Add the quinoa and reduce the heat to low. Cover and cook for 15 minutes.

Meanwhile, season the chicken with salt and black pepper.

In a large skillet, heat 2 to 3 tablespoons of the oil over medium heat. Add the chicken and cook for about 15 minutes, until cooked through. Remove the chicken from the pan and cut it into bite-size pieces.

Transfer the cooked quinoa to a medium bowl and fluff it with a fork. Add the chicken and bell pepper and stir gently to combine.

In a container with a tight-fitting lid, combine the remaining ½ cup oil, the vinegar, garlic, mustard, oregano, basil, and ½ teaspoon salt. Seal the container and shake well to combine.

Pour the dressing over the quinoa salad and toss to coat. Refrigerate until cool. When ready to serve, place ½ cup of the spinach in each bowl and scoop quinoa salad over the top.

Cool Confetti Rice and Chicken Bowls

Serves 6

This salad is similar to the Quinoa Salad on page 167 in that it packs well, holds up for a few days in the refrigerator, and adds a lot of variety to your packed lunch or dinner. Use any method you like for cooking the brown rice. I like to use the pressure cooker—1¼ cups water, 1 cup brown rice, and a cook time of 17 minutes yields fantastic rice.

1 pound chicken tenders

Salt and black pepper

½ cup plus 2 to 3 tablespoons olive oil

3 cups cooked brown rice

1 red bell pepper, chopped

1 cup frozen corn kernels, thawed

1 carrot, diced

¼ cup diced green onions (scallions)

¼ cup red wine vinegar

½ teaspoon dry mustard

1 garlic clove, crushed

Season the chicken with salt and black pepper.

In a large skillet, heat 2 to 3 tablespoons of the oil over medium heat. Add the chicken and cook for about 15 minutes, until cooked through. Remove the chicken from the skillet and cut it into bite-size pieces.

In a large bowl, stir together the chicken, rice, bell pepper, corn, carrot, and green onions.

In a container with a tight-fitting lid, combine the remaining ½ cup oil, the vinegar, dry mustard, ½ teaspoon salt, ¼ teaspoon pepper, and the garlic. Seal the container and shake well to mix.

Pour the dressing over the chicken mixture and toss to combine. Cover and refrigerate until cool.

Jambon-Beurre French Picnic

Serves 4

When Jim and I visited Paris, one of the first things we did was make our way to the top of the Eiffel Tower. Elevators shuttled us to the summit, but we opted to walk back down. By the time we made it down to the first level, which is still surprisingly high, we'd worked up an appetite. Even though we knew there were probably much better restaurants nearby, we opted for the sandwich stand in the Eiffel Tower and a table overlooking that beautiful Paris view. The *jambon-beurre* (simple ham sandwiches, sometimes with cheese, on baguettes spread with butter) were good, but were made even better by the setting and the fact that we were sharing the moment together. Baguettes tend to be sturdy, so these sandwiches pack well. Pair them with grapes, apples, or a simple green salad for an easy picnic.

1 (24-inch) baguette

1 to 2 tablespoons salted European butter or regular salted butter, at room temperature

8 ounces sliced deli ham

4 slices baby Swiss cheese or Gruyère cheese

Slice the baguette crosswise into four equal pieces and halve each of those pieces lengthwise. Spread butter over the inside cut surfaces of each baguette. Divide the ham evenly among the baguettes. Top with the cheese, close the sandwiches, and serve.

I WANT TO MAKE SOMETHING EXTRA TONIGHT

When I'm in a hurry, my focus is always on the main dish, but side dishes serve more purpose than just giving you more food to eat. They can help round out the nutrition of your meal, balance the flavors, and complement or contrast the color and texture of the main dish.

With some planning, you can be a pro at pairing main dishes and side dishes. Pair spicy main dishes with sides that are milder in flavor. Creamy comfort-food recipes can be paired with sides that have a stronger flavor. Try tomatoes that are a bit acidic or dark green vegetables like Brussels sprouts or turnip greens that have a stronger taste.

Consider the texture of the recipe. Soft dishes like pasta pair well with crunchy sides such as salads. Soup and crackers, eggs and toast, grilled cheese and tomato soup—all of these classic combos work in part because of the way the textures play off each other.

Color is very important in creating good food. A plate of salmon, cauliflower, and mashed potatoes isn't very inspiring to look at. The salmon will look and taste much better when paired with broccoli and a baked sweet potato.

Side dishes are also a great place to bring plenty of vegetables into the mix. When you're in a hurry, a simple green salad, carrot sticks, or apple slices work great. If you have a little more time, try some of these recipes. They are all simple to make, but will have a big impact on your meal.

Power Chopped Salad

Serves 8 to 10

If you've been looking for a way to eat your veggies and love them, try this salad. The addition of the dried fruit and the bit of honey in the dressing make it scrumptious, while all the good-for-you veggies pack a healthy punch. This makes a very large bowl, but it holds up really well for several days in the fridge. It's perfect for packing, too.

1 small bunch kale, finely chopped

1 small head cauliflower, finely chopped

2 carrots, finely chopped

¼ cup chopped pecans

½ cup dried cherries or cranberries

3 tablespoons honey

1 tablespoon lemon juice

2 tablespoons white wine vinegar

Salt and black pepper

Put the kale, cauliflower, and carrots in a large bowl. Add the pecans and dried cherries to the bowl. Drizzle the salad with the honey, lemon juice, and vinegar and season with salt and pepper. Toss to coat everything with the dressing and serve.

Bahamian Johnny Cake

Makes one 8 x 8-inch cake

This recipe came to me from Elsa, who also gave me her recipe for Bahamian Chicken Souse (page 54). Traditionally, Bahamian Johnny Cake doesn't have cornmeal or coconut milk in it, but Elsa's version contains both. As happens so often, as recipes are passed through various cooks and generations, they change. I love this about the cooking and sharing process. If you'd rather make a pan of sweetened cornbread instead, you only need to swap out the coconut milk for regular milk and drop the vanilla and nutmeg from the ingredients.

Vegetable oil spray or butter, for greasing

1 cup yellow cornmeal

1 cup all-purpose flour

¼ cup sugar

1 tablespoon baking powder

½ teaspoon salt

⅛ teaspoon ground nutmeg

4 tablespoons (½ stick) salted butter, melted, plus butter for serving

1 large egg

1 cup full-fat coconut milk

1 teaspoon vanilla extract

Preheat the oven to 425°F. Grease an 8-inch square baking pan with vegetable oil spray or butter.

In a medium bowl, stir together the cornmeal, flour, sugar, baking powder, salt, and nutmeg. Add the melted butter, egg, coconut milk, and vanilla and stir until well combined. Pour the batter into the prepared pan. Bake for 20 to 25 minutes.

Slice and serve hot, with butter.

Red Onion and Orange Salad

Serves 4

I know red onion and orange sounds like a very strange combination, but stick with me. This is the most amazing-tasting salad. It's more method than recipe, but it's so much more than the sum of its parts. If you're trying it for the first time, follow these proportions, which make enough for four people. The sharp taste of the onion contrasts nicely with the sweet citrus flavor of the orange. The flavor is so bright that it seems like it's been tossed with a dressing, but the only seasoning used is salt and pepper. This is a great side dish for chicken or fish, and it won't leave you scrambling for additional pots or wrangling too many other ingredients like many side dishes do.

4 oranges

¼ cup thinly sliced red onion

Kosher salt and black pepper

Peel the oranges and cut them into bite-size pieces. Transfer them to a bowl and toss with the red onion. Season with salt and pepper and serve immediately.

Southern-Style Skillet Greens with Cider Vinegar

Serves 6 to 8

Greens have made a big comeback in recent years because they're so nutritious. If you're still a bit skeptical, you're not alone. When I was in high school, I worked at a cafeteria that served greens that were cooked down to what one older gentleman laughingly called "silage," after what's found in the bottom of a silo of grain. That's not very appetizing! I promise that this recipe is nothing like that. Instead of cooking the greens nearly past recognition, this recipe wilts them until they're tender, but not mushy. Seasoned with onion, garlic, and cider vinegar, this side is vegetarian and healthy!

2 to 3 tablespoons olive oil

2 garlic cloves, crushed

1 onion, diced

1 pound greens (collard, kale, mustard, turnip, or a combination)

2 tablespoons cider vinegar

In a large skillet, heat the oil over medium heat. Add the garlic and onion and cook for about 5 minutes, until the onion is soft. Add some of the greens and ¼ cup water. Cook, letting the greens wilt, until there's room to add more. Continue adding greens and letting them wilt down between batches until you've fit them all in the skillet. Cook for 5 minutes more, until the greens are tender-crisp.

Stir in the vinegar and serve.

Little Black Dress Roasted Vegetables

My favorite way to cook vegetables is to roast them. This method makes every vegetable taste really good—even those you think you don't like. There's something about the roasting process that really brings out the flavors. Usually I use fresh vegetables for roasting, but both green beans and sugar snap peas can be roasted from frozen and still turn out great. You can also roast a variety of vegetables on one pan; just start with those that require more time in the oven and add the others later.

I like to keep the seasonings very simple to let the flavors of the veggies shine through. A drizzle of olive oil and sprinkle of salt and pepper will make any vegetable taste great, but feel free to play around with other seasonings too.

QUICK-ROASTING VEGETABLES (15 TO 20 MINUTES)

Brussels sprouts, halved or quartered, if large

Broccoli, cut into florets

Green beans, ends removed

Zucchini or yellow squash, cut into rounds or spears

Tomatoes, halved or quartered if large

Red bell peppers, cut into 2-inch pieces

Cabbage, cut into wedges through the core

SLOWER-ROASTING VEGETABLES (25 TO 35 MINUTES)

Onions, quartered or sliced

Celery, cut into 2-inch pieces

Fennel, bulb quartered and cut into ¼-inch-thick slices

Potatoes, cut into thick wedges or 2-inch cubes

Sweet potatoes, cut into thick wedges or 2-inch cubes

Butternut squash, cut into 2-inch cubes

Beets, peeled and cut into ¼-inch slices

Carrots, cut into 2-inch pieces

Parsnips, cut into 2-inch pieces

Olive oil

Salt and black pepper, or other seasonings (optional)

Preheat the oven to 425°F.

Drizzle the vegetables with olive oil and sprinkle with salt and pepper or any other seasoning you like. Spread the vegetables in a single layer on a rimmed baking sheet and roast until fork-tender and browned.

Best-Ever Roasted Sweet Potatoes with Ginger, Cinnamon, and Thyme

Serves 6 to 8

You know how church potlucks can have the best food sometimes? A few years ago, someone brought a sweet potato dish that had me going back for seconds and thirds. I asked for the recipe and found that it wasn't difficult, but it was a little time-consuming. I simplified it by tossing the sweet potatoes with the seasonings in the recipe and then roasting them. This is now my favorite way to make sweet potatoes.

3 sweet potatoes, scrubbed and cut into 1-inch cubes

2 to 3 tablespoons olive oil, plus more for greasing the pan

1 teaspoon kosher salt

⅛ teaspoon black pepper

½ teaspoon dried thyme

¼ teaspoon ground ginger

¼ teaspoon ground cinnamon

Preheat the oven to 400°F. Grease a rimmed baking sheet with oil.

Place the sweet potatoes in a large bowl. Drizzle with the oil and sprinkle with the salt, pepper, thyme, ginger, and cinnamon. Toss to coat the sweet potatoes with the oil and spices. Spread the sweet potatoes in a single layer on the prepared baking sheet. Bake for 25 minutes, until the sweet potatoes are tender when pierced with a fork.

Honey-Sriracha Roasted Brussels Sprouts

Serves 4 to 6

My eldest daughter told me about this side dish, which she'd eaten at a local restaurant. I decided it sounded like a great recipe to try at home. If you haven't tried roasted Brussels sprouts, you must! I didn't think I liked Brussels sprouts at all until I tried them roasted. This recipe dresses up the roasted sprouts a bit more. The sriracha gives them just a bit of heat that contrasts with the sweet honey. Feel free to adjust the amount of sriracha to suit your family's tastes. I don't like food to be too spicy, and I found the tablespoon of sriracha called for here to be the right amount for me. If you like more or less heat, adjust accordingly.

1 to 2 tablespoons olive oil, plus more for greasing the pan

1 pound Brussels sprouts, halved

½ teaspoon salt

¼ cup honey

1 tablespoon sriracha

Preheat the oven to 425°F. Grease a rimmed baking sheet with oil.

Place the Brussels sprouts in a large bowl. Drizzle them with the oil and sprinkle with the salt. Spread them in an even layer over the prepared baking sheet and bake for 15 minutes.

Meanwhile, in a small bowl, stir together the honey and sriracha.

After 15 minutes, pull the pan from the oven and drizzle the honey-sriracha over the sprouts. Toss to coat and pop them back in the oven for 5 minutes more.

Loaded Smashed Potatoes

Serves 6

There are some side dishes that are able to take center stage. This is one of them. You can serve these alongside the simplest main dish—a grilled chicken breast or piece of fish—or pair them with Mexican Meat Loaf (page 146). These creamy potatoes are loaded with sour cream and cheddar cheese and topped with bacon and green onions.

1½ pounds baby red potatoes, unpeeled

1 teaspoon kosher salt

Black pepper

1 (8-ounce) container sour cream

1 cup shredded cheddar cheese

1 to 2 tablespoons milk, if needed

4 bacon slices, cooked and crumbled

2 green onions (scallions), sliced

Put the potatoes in a large pot and add water to cover. Bring the water to a boil and cook until the potatoes are very tender and fall apart easily, about 30 minutes. Drain the potatoes and place them in the bowl of a stand mixer fitted with the paddle attachment. Run the mixer on medium-low speed to smash the potatoes but leave some pieces—you don't want them to be mashed smooth. Stir in the salt, pepper to taste, sour cream, and cheddar cheese until well combined. If the potatoes seem a little too dry, stir in the milk, 1 tablespoon at a time.

Top each serving with the crumbled bacon and green onions.

I HAVE A SWEET TOOTH TONIGHT

In all truth, I don't just have a sweet tooth tonight. I have one every night! I love desserts of all kinds. Ice cream is my favorite, but I can go for any sweet at any time. For years, dessert was a daily thing in our house. Everyone in my family can make chocolate chip cookies without looking at a recipe. One of our friends joked that we didn't know you don't have to eat those cookies straight from the oven. When you've got four kids in or around their teen years, it's possible to polish off a lot of cookies at once!

I've reined in my sweet habit lately, but that doesn't mean I don't still love a good treat. You'll find recipes in this chapter that will work for a dinner with company, a potluck, a bake sale contribution, or even as a sweet tooth quick-fix.

I hope you'll enjoy them as much as I do!

Balsamic Strawberries over Vanilla Shortcakes with Fresh Basil

Serves 8

If you're not sure about the balsamic vinegar and basil in this recipe, let me encourage you to give it a try. The balsamic vinegar brings out the depth of flavor in the berries, and the fresh basil lends a surprising brightness to the dessert. Of course, you can skip both of those ingredients and still be very happy with the result! Who wouldn't be happy with strawberry shortcake? But give the recipe a try as written, because I think you'll like it.

FOR THE SHORTCAKES

2 cups all-purpose flour, plus more for dusting

2 tablespoons baking powder

1 teaspoon salt

¼ cup sugar

5 tablespoons salted butter, softened

1 teaspoon vanilla

¾ cup milk

FOR THE BERRIES

4 to 6 cups sliced fresh strawberries

½ cup sugar

1 tablespoon balsamic vinegar

TO SERVE

Vanilla ice cream

Handful of fresh basil, coarsely chopped

For the shortcakes, preheat the oven to 450°F.

In a large bowl, combine the flour, baking powder, salt, and sugar. Cut in the butter to form soft crumbs. Add vanilla and milk and stir gently to combine. Flour a work surface and turn the dough out onto the flour. Pat the dough into a 1-inch thickness. Use a biscuit cutter or a 2½-inch-diameter glass to cut biscuits from the dough. Place the biscuits on a baking sheet. Bake for 10 to 11 minutes.

Meanwhile, for the strawberries, in a small bowl, stir together the strawberries, sugar, and vinegar. Allow the strawberries to macerate until they are softened and soaked in liquid.

Split the shortcakes in half horizontally. Top the bottom halves with the strawberries, ice cream, and basil, finish with the top halves, and serve immediately.

Easiest Peanut Butter and Jelly Bars

Makes one 8-inch square pan

One of my crazy dreams is to quit everything, rent a hole-in-the-wall space, and open a PB&J restaurant. I would do nothing but make and sell homemade peanut butter, jams, and freshly baked breads. And if I do ever take on that crazy dream, you can bet these bars will be on the dessert menu. You can use any type of jam you like in these, but my favorite is strawberry. The only downside is that you're going to need to wait for these to cool before eating them. They really do taste better cool, so it's worth the wait, but I suggest hiding them from the rest of the family. And maybe even from yourself!

¾ cup (1½ sticks) plus 1 tablespoon salted butter, at room temperature

1½ cups quick-cooking oats

1 cup packed light brown sugar

1½ cups all-purpose flour

1 teaspoon baking powder

½ teaspoon salt

¾ cup smooth peanut butter

1½ to 1¾ cups jam (any kind)

Preheat the oven to 350°F. Grease an 8-inch square baking pan with 1 tablespoon of the butter.

In the bowl of a stand mixer fitted with the paddle attachment, combine the remaining ¾ cup (1½ sticks) butter, the oats, brown sugar, flour, baking powder, salt, and peanut butter. Beat on medium speed, stopping to scrape down the sides of the bowl as needed, until well combined.

Press half the dough into the prepared pan. Spread the jam over the first dough layer, then top with the remaining dough, pressing it lightly into an even layer with your hands. Bake for 30 to 40 minutes. Let cool completely on a wire rack before slicing and serving.

Skillet Peach Crisp

Serves 4 to 6

Have you ever made a recipe and then declared yourself a genius because it was so good? That's exactly what I did when I made this Skillet Peach Crisp for friends. When you make this, you'll declare yourself a genius, too! Besides the fact that it is delicious, this dessert is just so easy and quick to make. It starts with frozen peach slices, so the prep is simple and you can enjoy it any time of year. An ovenproof skillet keeps the cooking time quick. Don't worry if you don't have a skillet that can go under the broiler—there's a workaround for that (see Note). Just be sure to make this one soon, so you can enjoy the bubbling sweet peaches mingled with the buttery, crisp topping. Serve it with scoops of vanilla ice cream.

5 tablespoons salted butter

1 (16-ounce) bag frozen peach slices, thawed

¼ cup granulated sugar

½ cup quick-cooking oats

½ cup packed light brown sugar

¼ cup all-purpose flour

¼ cup chopped pecans

½ teaspoon ground cinnamon

Vanilla ice cream, for serving

Preheat the broiler.

In a 9- or 10-inch ovenproof skillet, melt 1 tablespoon of the butter over medium heat. Add the peaches and granulated sugar and cook, stirring, until the peaches soften, 10 to 12 minutes.

Meanwhile, in a medium bowl, stir together the oats, brown sugar, flour, pecans, and cinnamon. Add the remaining 4 tablespoons butter, using a fork to cut the butter into the dry ingredients to form coarse crumbs. Add half the crumbs to the skillet with the peaches and stir to combine. Spread the remaining crumbs over the top of the peaches. Pop the skillet into the oven and broil for 1 to 2 minutes to brown the top of the crisp.

Serve warm, with scoops of vanilla ice cream.

NOTE If you don't have an ovenproof skillet, use a regular skillet to cook the peaches. Add half the topping, then pour the mixture into a buttered 2-quart casserole dish and sprinkle the rest of the topping over the peaches. Broil as directed to finish.

Lemon Cheesecake Dip

Makes about 3 cups

This simple dip will have you and your guests coming back to the bowl again and again. My favorite way to serve this is with gingersnap cookies. Lemon and ginger is a fantastic flavor combination. I often make a recipe for warm gingerbread with lemon sauce in the winter. This Lemon Cheesecake Dip brings those same flavors together in a way that's perfect for warmer weather. Try dipping strawberries into the dip for a summer treat.

1 (8-ounce) package cream cheese, at room temperature (see Note, page 2)

1 cup confectioners' sugar

1 (10-ounce) jar prepared lemon curd

1 (5.3-ounce) container plain Greek yogurt

Gingersnaps, strawberries, or other sliced fruit, for serving

In a large bowl using a handheld mixer, beat the cream cheese and confectioners' sugar together until smooth. Fold in the lemon curd and yogurt by hand. Cover and refrigerate for at least 1 hour or until chilled.

Serve with gingersnaps, strawberries, or other sliced fruit for dipping.

Cherry Vanilla Ice Cream

Serves 6

Ice cream is my favorite dessert, and I love to make it at home. This recipe works well in a countertop-style ice cream maker. These appliances make ice cream-making so easy, but you can also use a more traditional ice-and-rock-salt-type ice cream maker. Just be sure to double the recipe, since those canisters hold more. You'll also want to add the dark sweet cherries with the other ingredients instead of waiting until the end to add them. It's much easier to add mix-in ingredients with the countertop-style makers than the traditional type. No matter what type of maker you use, you won't believe how easy it is to stir this recipe together. No need to cook and cool. You're just five ingredients away from delicious homemade ice cream!

3 ounces cream cheese, at room temperature (see Note, page 2)

1 (14-ounce) can sweetened condensed milk

2 teaspoons vanilla extract

2 cups half-and-half

6 ounces frozen dark sweet cherries, thawed and coarsely chopped

In a large bowl with a spout, stir together the cream cheese and condensed milk until well combined. Stir in the vanilla and half-and-half, making sure everything is well combined. Pour the mixture into an ice cream maker and freeze according to the manufacturer's instructions. (This should take about 30 minutes for a countertop-style ice cream maker.) Once the ice cream has finished churning, add the cherries and allow the maker to blend them through the ice cream. Serve immediately for a soft serve–style ice cream, or transfer the ice cream to a freezer-safe container, cover, and freeze until ready to serve.

No-Bake Coconut Cheesecake

Serves 8

You only need six ingredients for this simple dessert, and that includes making the crust. This one really is as easy as pie. The hardest part will be waiting for it to chill so you can eat it. For the crust use either regular graham cracker crumbs, or give the cheesecake a chocolate twist by using chocolate grahams. You'll find cream of coconut near the alcoholic drink mixes in the grocery. Used for making piña coladas and dessert, cream of coconut is sweetened with an intense coconut flavor.

1¼ cups graham cracker crumbs, regular or chocolate

¼ cup sugar

⅓ cup salted butter, melted

1 (8-ounce) package cream cheese, at room temperature (see Note, page 2)

1 (15-ounce) can cream of coconut

½ cup sweetened flaked coconut

In a small bowl, stir together the graham cracker crumbs, sugar, and melted butter. Pour the mixture into a pie plate and press the crumbs over the bottom and up the sides of the plate. Freeze the crust for 10 minutes.

Meanwhile, in a large bowl using a handheld mixer, beat together the cream cheese and cream of coconut until well blended. Fold in the flaked coconut by hand.

Remove the crust from the freezer and pour in the filling. Cover and refrigerate for at least 6 hours or up to overnight before slicing and serving.

Chocolate-Cinnamon Crumb Cake

Makes one 9 x 9-inch cake

This simple coffee cake recipe is a chocolaty take on one that my mom has made for as long as I can remember. The cinnamon flavor is only hinted at in each bite, but there's no mistaking the chocolate. No need to get out a mixer—this one gets stirred together with a spoon, making it simple and easy. It can be served any time you need a quick dessert, or add it to your breakfast or brunch menu for a morning treat. It's equally good served warm or cool.

Vegetable oil spray or butter, for greasing the pan

1½ cups all-purpose flour

½ cup unsweetened cocoa powder

1 cup packed light brown sugar

2½ teaspoons baking powder

1 teaspoon ground cinnamon

½ teaspoon salt

¾ cup (1½ sticks) salted butter, at room temperature

2 large eggs, beaten

½ cup milk

Preheat the oven to 350°F. Grease a 9-inch square baking pan with vegetable oil spray or butter.

In a large bowl, stir together the flour, cocoa powder, brown sugar, baking powder, cinnamon, and salt. Add the butter and cut it in with a fork or pastry blender until the mixture forms coarse crumbs. Scoop out ½ cup of the crumbs and set aside to use for the topping.

Add the beaten eggs and milk to the crumbs remaining in the bowl and stir to combine. Spoon the batter into the prepared pan. Sprinkle the reserved crumbs evenly over the top. Bake for 30 minutes.

Serve warm or at room temperature.

Apricot Almond Cookies

Makes 5 to 6 dozen cookies

In my mind, these are perfect cookies. They're soft, with chewy apricots, crunchy almonds, and creamy white chocolate baking chips. The dough that holds it all together has a nutty flavor that keeps them from being too sweet. As a bonus, these can be gluten-free if you use gluten-free oats.

¾ cup almond butter

½ cup (1 stick) salted butter, at room temperature

2 large eggs

1 teaspoon vanilla extract

½ cup granulated sugar

½ cup packed light brown sugar

2½ cups quick-cooking oats

2 teaspoons baking soda

1 (11-ounce) bag white chocolate baking chips

6 ounces dried apricots, chopped

⅔ cup sliced almonds

Preheat the oven to 350°F.

In the bowl of a stand mixer fitted with the paddle attachment, beat together the almond butter and butter on medium speed until well blended. Add the eggs and vanilla and beat to combine. Beat in the granulated sugar and brown sugar until well combined.

In a small bowl, stir the oats and baking soda together. With the mixer running on medium-low speed, gradually add the oats to the butter mixture and mix until combined. Stir in the baking chips, apricots, and almonds by hand. Drop the dough by tablespoons onto a baking sheet, spacing the dollops of dough 2 inches apart. Bake for 10 to 12 minutes, until golden brown.

Transfer the cookies to a wire rack to cool.

GRATITUDE

———

Every morning as part of my routine, I write down at least three things I'm thankful for. The names here were part of my morning lists multiple times while I was writing this book.

Thank you to my family: To Jim, my husband, who has always encouraged me and cheered me on. To Meredith, Stephen, Peter, Kate, Isaac, and Mia, who have done so much taste-testing! I love the dinner traditions we've shared together.

Thank you to those who helped with the book writing: To Maria Ribas, my literary agent, who worked with me to develop this from an idea into a full book. To Susan Tjaden, my editor, who has been a dream to work with. Thanks also to Meredith Garrison and Mary Beth Brannon for your help in cleaning up the first draft of the manuscript, and to Beth Moore, my assistant, who helped me organize and thank everyone who tested recipes. To Kate Sabella, for her help with the grocery lists in the book.

To the many people who have read my blog over the years: Your feedback and support have meant the world to me.

INDEX

Get free meal plans and grocery lists using the recipes in this book at eatathometonight.com/plans.